Cabin Fever on Noah's Ark

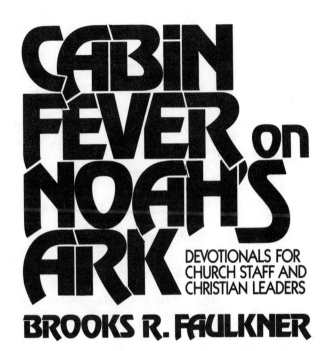

CABIN FEVER on NOAH'S ARK

DEVOTIONALS FOR CHURCH STAFF AND CHRISTIAN LEADERS

BROOKS R. FAULKNER

BROADMAN PRESS
NASHVILLE, TENNESSEE

Unless otherwise noted, all Scripture quotations are taken from the Holy Bible, *New International Version,* copyright © 1973, 1978, 1984 by International Bible Society.

All Scripture quotations marked (KJV) are from the *King James Version* of the Bible.

All Scripture quotations marked (NASB) are from the *New American Standard Bible.* © The Lockman Foundation, 1960, 1962, 1963, 1968, 1971, 1972, 1973, 1975, 1977. Used by permission.

All Scripture quotations marked (GNB) are from the *Good News Bible,* the Bible in Today's English Version. Old Testament: Copyright © American Bible Society 1976; New Testament: Copyright © American Bible Society 1966, 1971, 1976. Used by permission.

Library of Congress Cataloging-in-Publication Data

Faulkner, Brooks R.

   Cabin fever on Noah's ark / Brooks R. Faulkner.

     p. cm.

   ISBN 0-8054-6046-2

   1. Clergy—Prayer-books and devotions—English. 2. Church officers—Prayer-books and devotions—English. 3. Devotional calendars. I. Title.

BV4011.6.F38   1991

242'.692—dc20

                                   90-25403

                                   CIP

To Brook Hollow Baptist Church, Nashville, Tennessee

Contents

Introduction

After 150 days, Noah and his family were sick of each other. They were confined. They had "cabin fever." But, it was better than the storm and flood outside. They had to adjust. They needed patience and tolerance. They also needed a change. Ministers are like that. They lead the spiritual journey for others. But, they can get sick of each other, too. They can get sick of church members. They can get cabin fever, but it's still better than the alternative.

This series of devotionals is an "inside look," written with the purpose of rediscovering the sense of wonder and mystery of the Christian faith. It's written for pastors, church staff members, and other church leaders. Each of these audiences has unique spiritual needs—not more than others, not less, but unique. Our familiarity with devotional ideas tends to create some cynicism with trite, spiritual clichés for us. We need fresh, spiritual eye-openers.

Ministers and church leaders are isolated. We spend much energy leading the devotional life of others. So much, in fact, that depletion slips in on us. I can use the word *us* with integrity because it has happened to me. I get so hungry to be fed spiritually.

I need a devotional guide designed specifically for my needs as a minister. I suspect most church staff members do. This book was born out of that need.

1

Cabin Fever on Noah's Ark

"But God remembered Noah and all the wild animals and the livestock that were with him in the ark, and he sent a wind over the earth" (Gen. 8:1).

" 'Do you think Nietzsche was correct when he said that we have murdered God?'
"He went further than that and said we have murdered Him and this is the most glorious event in human history.
. . . The poor fellow [Nietzsche] in his loony bin in Venice is a subject for compassion obviously."[1]

Richard Broholm, author of *The Man of Faith in the New Age,* once told a chapel audience: "The church is a lot like Noah's Ark—if not for the storm outside, you couldn't stand the smell inside."

Noah was 600. He was both righteous and blameless. He "walked with God" (Gen. 6:9). Three excellent credentials for saving the world, don't you think?

The people, on the other hand, were not righteous, blameless, nor did they walk with God. To be sure, the earth was "corrupt in God's sight" and was "full of violence" (v. 11), not unlike our earth today.

Therefore, God set Noah about the task of faith. The ark was 450 feet by 75 feet by 45 feet. It was large—one and one-half football fields or forty-five basketball courts in length. It had three decks. The Lenai deck was the most plush. That was where the people were. It was on top. The Rose deck was for the small animals. The Club deck was for the heavy animals—elephants, hippos, horses, cows, and so forth. God told Noah to take seven of every kind of clean animal, two of every kind of unclean animal.

Shem, Ham, and Japheth can thank their lucky stars they had a good dad. They rode the coattail of his righteousness and blamelessness.

It rained and rained for forty days and nights. Genesis 7:22-23 suggested in cryptic terms the extent of the damage. "Everything . . . on the face of the earth was wiped out."

The boat ride was 150 days—more than twenty-one weeks. It is true they were on the top deck, but I am sure they were grateful for the "wind" that God sent. The family got sick of each other. They had cabin fever.

Mount Ararat, which had been covered by at least twenty feet of water during the flood, was dry enough to land on.

No one knows for sure where Noah landed, but prominent names in theology, science, and even astronomy have given search. No substantiated proof has been found.

For years I missed the apparent heart of this wonderful story. I considered the good versus evil conflict—an evil earth and a good man. I did not consider thoroughly the covenant God made with Noah after the flood. "I will demand an accounting from every animal. And from each man, too, I will demand an accounting for the life of his fellow man" (Gen. 9:5).

The sign of the new covenant was a rainbow.

If I had to give a moral to this story adapted to today, it would be: "At the End of Every Smelly Situation in a Church, There's a Rainbow." It's a little hokey, but it's true. Cabin fever makes you appreciate the freedom of the outside. However, you forget the good that is inside when you have cabin fever.

The odor may linger, but the rainbow makes it fade into oblivion.

There are three parts to this devotional.

1. The corruption was real.
2. Most everyone needs space.
3. God will bless the righteous and blameless.

The Corruption Was Real

Friedrich Wilhelm Nietzsche had a brilliant mind. His works *The Will to Power* and *Thus Spake Zarathustra* were required reading in many college and seminary courses because they shaped much of the history of World Wars I and II. He influenced Hitler. His cry was "God is dead. Long live Superman."[2] Much of the evil that has raised its ugly head in this century is in direct proportion to arrogant intellectuals who proclaim the absence of God. Nietzsche looked "within" himself to find the cure for human miseries. Ultimately, although complicated with a variety of illnesses, he was committed to an institution for mental incompetence. There he finished many of his most famous works. He could not find the replacement for God within himself. The story repeats itself. People keep looking within. The search leads to self-indulgence, selfishness, narcissism, and corruption. The search is an exercise in the futility of violence.

Alexander Solzhenitsyn said in an address at Harvard that our social structure is tumbling because of our idolatry of health, wealth, and happiness.[3]

Turn on cable television. One channel has health tips, another a lecture on taking care of your body, a third on how to make quick money, and still another a panel discussing how to be happy by standing up for yourself. All are good, but we sometimes worship them—these idolatrous beings of health, wealth, and happiness.

Does the story repeat itself? I think so. We have arks to build. Indeed, there is corruption.

Most Everyone Needs Space

Wherever two or three are gathered in Christ's name, you can be assured that one of them is thinking about starting another church. People just have a tough time getting along when things get close. After all, it had been 150 days. They were all getting cabin fever. The animals were restless. It's a common malady in churches. We get so preoccupied with our own administration that we forget to get outside and do God's work. We know everyone needs some space. Sometimes we make allowances. Frequently, we do not.

Vance Havner once asked a group of ministers, "Don't you find it strange that when we get disgusted in a church we pray for a change of church fields rather than a change of character?" The smell in the church will occasionally be difficult to live with, but remember the storm outside.

What kind of people makes it difficult for us and creates our need for space?

Judgmental People

The very nature of the Christian who is committed to his or her church is judicial. We feel guilty because we have sinned. We know what our sin is. We confess our sin, experience God's forgiveness, but the cycle begins again. We are quick to judge ourselves, but we are often quicker to judge others.

We scream to all those around us in our churches, "Don't judge me!" The closeness in the ark is enhanced when others would make us responsible. Judicial people are a pain. Religious judicial people are impossible. The worst are those who think they speak for God when they criticize people.

Relatives

Distance with relatives is essential for getting along. All the people on Lenai deck were relatives. In some smaller churches almost all are kinfolk.

Familiarity breeds contempt, especially in families. You're close enough to smell the garlic, hear the whining, feel the expectations to bring home more, do more, and be there more often. You find negative thoughts surfacing about the most important people in your life. Ham, Shem, Japheth, and their families brought a lot of grief to Noah and Mrs. Noah, and vice versa.

Second-Guessers

Consider this scenario. Ham said on the fourth day out on the ark, "Are you sure we're doing the right thing?"

Noah said, "No, but based on the best information we have, we are. God has spoken and I have listened." In the modern-day context, a minister recommends the calling of a minister of education. He feels he is doing the right thing. It is risky. However, based on the best information, he recommends. Second-guessers will be there. Sometimes they are right, making it even more infuriating. They will be there, right or wrong.

In 1989, the University of Tennessee basketball team beat Vanderbilt University by one point! Vanderbilt missed two free throw opportunities in the last seventeen seconds. We lost. They won. I kept thinking, *What if* . . . Wasted energy! Second-guessing is disruptive and frustrating—especially to church staff persons. And especially if we are wrong. Noah was right. Frequently, we do not have that luxury.

Gotcha People

No one is more difficult to live with than the vindictive person who is waiting for the "right moment." These people are in every church. They get their feelings hurt and sometimes wait for years to get their retribution.

The sad part is that they often do not know they are vindictive. They are vindicated in their vindictiveness because the victim deserves it.

Occasionally you begin to hear statements like: "Watch your back!" "Be careful what you say." "They're lying in wait." Gotcha people are hard to live with. Unfortunately, those occasional statements you hear about "gotcha people" are good advice and should be heeded.

God Will Bless the Righteous and Blameless

There is a rainbow. God will not leave us hanging forever, although it often feels as if He does.

The rainbow is God's promise. Things may be close, but there is a rainbow. There are judgmental people, but there is a rainbow. There are relatives who are with us too much, but there is a rainbow. There are second-guessers, but there is a rainbow. There are gotcha people, but there is a rainbow. The corruption of this world can not contend with the blessing of God.

Gary Morris sang a lovely song:

> Give her the thorns and she'll find the roses;
> Give her the sand and she'll find the sea;
> Give her the rain and she'll find the rainbow;
> Look what she's done for me.

One hundred fifty days may be five years in a desolate church of loveless people, but with God's blessing it can change the people. God will not leave us comfortless. The rainbow is the promise of God. Cabin fever is worth the wait. There is hope in the face of dismal feelings of failure because His mission is larger than ours.

Notes

1. Malcolm Muggeridge, *The End of Christendom* (Grand Rapids: Wm. B. Eerdmans Publishing Co., 1980), 26.

2. Friedrich Wilhelm Nietzsche, *Thus Spake Zarathustra,* part I, section 7, in *Complete Works,* ed. Oscar Long (Edinburg: T. N. Forelis, 1909), 207.

3. Alexander Solzheintsyn, "A World Split Apart," Commencement Address at Harvard, June 8, 1978 (New York: Harper and Row, 1978), 47-51.

2

Comfort Amidst Uncertainty

"Only a peace between equals can last."[1]

"All my friends are waiting for me to slip" (Jer. 20:10).

He was facing a great deal of criticism from some church members. Only a few, he admitted. The impact of criticism made him feel like the "some" were "many" instead of a "few."

Eighteen months earlier he had seen the same signs. A pastor-church relations committee, composed of a subcommittee of deacons, had brought a written list of demands for some changes in his behavior: (1) Take fewer actions before consulting appropriate church groups; (2) Purchase nothing over $100 without prior approval; (3) Have more one-on-one conversations with the church staff; and (4) Be more time conscious of the closing of worship services.

Now, the uncertainty had surfaced again. Had he lapsed back into old habits? Were the old adversaries angry again? He didn't know. He did, however, feel the impact of uncertainty. He knew if he didn't deal with the emotional tremors he was headed toward a spiritual earthquake. But how? How can we find comfort amidst uncertainty? Here are several suggestions:

Treat People with Respect

Some church members are easy to like. Some are difficult. Some are downright impossible.

Woodrow Wilson told the Senate, "Only a peace between equals can last." This was the thesis of his speech advocating the League of Nations. The isolationists defied him. They do so in churches as well.

Some church members, unfortunately, do not see church staff as equals. Some see church staff as less than equals. Some see church staff as more than equals.

Some see church staff as "enlisted military personnel." Some see church staff as four-star generals.

We must be considerate. We must see others as our equals, even those we don't particularly like.

Avoid Paranoia

Of course, some are really out to get us. That is not paranoia, but reality. The number of these persons is negligible in most churches.

It's been my experience that most deacons, leaders, and elders in churches are godly persons trying to do the best they can to serve with integrity and commitment. They don't deserve (for the most part) the abuse they occasionally receive in addresses in evangelism conferences, pastor and staff conferences, and state conventions.

Jeremiah said, "All my friends are waiting for me to slip" (Jer. 20:10). Dr. W. W. Adams, professor of biblical theology at The Southern Baptist Theological Seminary, told his students, "Jeremiah needed some new friends." Friends don't wait for you to slip. Enemies do.

Expect the best of friends. They will come through. You can find comfort even in uncertainty with real friends. They will support you. We do not have to be paranoid.

In the recesses of my mind, although I cannot document it, I remember a conversation:

Lucy: I don't need friends.
Charlie: I do. I need all the friends I can get.
Lucy: You try too hard, Charlie Brown.
Charlie: I'd even settle for a fair-weather friend.
Lucy: You should try to be more like me. I don't care if I have friends or not, just so I'm popular.
Charlie (as he walks away): I don't know. Talking to her never helps much.

With friends like Lucy, who wouldn't be paranoid?

Remember God Is Near

A few verses later God responds to Jeremiah. "'Am I only a God nearby,' declares the Lord, 'and not a God far away? Can anyone hide in secret places so that I cannot see him?' declares the Lord. 'Do not I fill heaven and earth?' declares the Lord" (Jer. 23:23-24).

During uncertainty, we are tempted to become convinced God is not nearby; He has forsaken us. No wonder we feel isolated. No wonder we can feel little comfort during uncertainty.

God says to Jeremiah, "Don't be ridiculous. I am near. I never left." When a demanding church member insists you should be two places at once, remember God is near. You can have comfort amidst uncertainty. When your personal budget is stretched with demands beyond your means, remember God is near. You can have comfort amidst uncertainty. When a spouse decides you have taken enough abuse from neurotics in the church, remember God is near. When it's no longer fun to go to the office because you're getting a cold shoulder . . . When it seems no one takes your advice in the religious education program . . . When you feel empty, tired, and frazzled, God is near. You can have comfort amidst uncertainty.

Note

1. Woodrow Wilson, *The World's Great Speeches,* ed. Lewis Copeland (Dover, N.Y.: Lawrence Lamm, 1941), 351.

3

Half Mystic, Half Mutt

"Man is a strange creature: half mystic and half mutt."

"If anyone wants to come with me he must forget himself, carry his cross, and follow me" (Matt. 16:24, GNB).

There are two stories in Matthew 16:16-20,21-18 about Peter, who was a lot like many of us.

In the first story Jesus *praised* Peter. In the second story He *reprimanded* Peter. In the first Jesus told Peter he had access to God. In the second Jesus told Peter he had access to the devil.

In the first Peter was called a "rock." In the second, he was called an "obstacle" (GNB).

In the first Jesus was questioning the disciples about who the people were saying that He was—John the Baptist, Elijah, and Jeremiah. "What about you?" Jesus asked.

That was when Peter made a historical declaration. "Thou art the Christ, the Son of the living God" (v. 16, KJV). Jesus was pleased. It's that kind of statement of faith that will be the foundation of the church. I am proud of you, Peter.

"Good answer. Good answer," said the cloud of witnesses.

However, almost in the same breath, Peter was an unruly and undisciplined disciple. It wasn't the first time and would not be the last.

The *Good News Bible* translates Jesus' response in an interesting manner: "Get away from me, Satan!" (v. 23).

All Peter had said was "God forbid it, Lord!" "That must never happen to you!" (v. 22). Peter loved Jesus. Jesus knew that. However, the irate spirit of Jesus suggests He might have been tempted to avoid the death He had predicted. Peter would protect Jesus. Peter's motives were *pure* but not *pleasing*.

Peter had a big mouth. He was habitually making promises he couldn't keep. Peter was the one who said "I will make three tents here, one for you, one for Moses, and one for Elijah" (Matt. 17:4, GNB). Remember, "I will make . . . ." The key was "I."

Peter was the one who pressed Jesus, "How many times do I have to forgive . . . ?" (Matt. 18:21, GNB). Again, the key was "I."

Peter was the one who said "I will never leave you, even though all the rest do!" And later "I will never say that even if I have to die with you!" (Matt. 26:33, 35, GNB). We're talking major foot-in-mouth disease.

It is etched in my memory. Margaret O'Brien was the young daughter of Edward G. Robinson. The name of the film is not pertinent. The scene is. Margaret O'Brien had been lost for hours. The floods came. The community was convinced O'Brien had been swept away in the floods along with another child. The search was frantic. After hours of uncertainty the two children showed up. They had disobeyed their parents and were afraid to go home.

Robinson picks up O'Brien. He hugs and kisses her. However, at the same time he was spanking her. He was overjoyed at her safety. He was angry with her disobedience. He walks across the bridge and through the crowd of people loving and spanking—both emotions at the same time. Half and half! Half mystic and half mutt! How is it possible?

I heard a story about a pastor who had embarrassingly confided to a friend that he sat during the choir special preparing to lead in worship through preaching and fighting impure thoughts about a woman in the choir. Half mystic and half mutt!

I have often found myself during the prayer in a worship service distracted by clichés and phrases that are apparently quoted from rote. I want to be spiritual. The fact that these words have been said thousands, even millions of times, is often disquieting and disconcerting. Half mystic and half mutt!

Where Does Half and Half Originate?

Simplistically, although certainly realistically and biblically, our half mystic and half mutt nature is seen best in "for all have sinned and fall short of the glory of God" (Rom. 3:23). We come by our half and half legitimately. We are human, not divine.

For centuries we have tried to be both selfless and selfish at the same time. Paul said it this way. "For I have the desire to do what is good, but I cannot carry it out. . . . So then, I myself in my mind am a slave to God's law, but in the sinful nature a slave to the law of sin" (Rom. 7:18b,25b).

The psychiatrist Harry Stack Sullivan gave birth to the phrases, but Daniel

Goleman develops the idea. According to Sullivan, there are three systems at work in the *half and half.*

(1) *Good-me,* which is enhanced by tenderness. This is who we like to think we are.

(2) *Bad-me,* which is enhanced by disapproval that gathers anxiety.

(3) *Not-me,* which is enhanced by denial. This is a way of dealing with "uncanny emotion" or feelings of dread and terror.

The half and half is the result of the first two functioning simultaneously—very much like Peter.

How Can the Christian Best Cope with the Half Mystic/Half Mutt Syndrome?

A poem I memorized in high school (the author long since forgotten) best illustrates this syndrome:

> The Padre', 'e says I'm a sinner.
> John Bull, 'e says I'm a saint.
> Both of 'em bound to be liars.
> I'm neither of 'em, I ain't.
> I'm a man, and a man is a mixture
> Right down from the day of his birth.
> Where a part of him come from heaven,
> And a part of him come from earth.

There you have it. We are not "little Christs" as some have contended. We are not even microcosms of Christ. We can aspire to be like Him. Jesus was from heaven: We are from earth, and God's grace gives us a little bit of heaven.

It is no accident that Jesus instructs Peter and us in Matthew 16:24-28:

Deny Yourself

We must deny the "mutt" and lift (good me) the mystic. All the hype from the early 1970s about letting our feelings out is just that: hype.

The biblical truth is that we must *filter.* We must turn destructive feelings into constructive feelings. We must take painful steps—disciplined, painful steps, to deny our sinful wants and fulfill the mission of Christ.

Take Up Your Cross

Competent scholars have studied that phrase for centuries. It is still difficult to translate. Perhaps Jesus was projecting His own sacrifice. Perhaps Jesus was saying to Peter, you will also face the cross. (According to tradition, Peter later requested "upside-down crucifixion.")

I think it meant know your "mutt" self and deal with it daily. *Know your limitations.* Don't delude yourself about your spiritual nature. You cannot put God in your pocket and say, "I have it now. I know what it takes." Learn daily. Grow daily. Search diligently. Pray without ceasing.

Follow Me

"Never Lord!" he said, "This shall never happen to you!" (Matt. 16:22). Peter did not want Jesus to die. Jesus Himself was sometimes uncertain. He prayed, "If it is possible, may this cup be taken from me. Yet not as I will but as you will" (Matt. 26:39).

"For whoever wants to save his life will lose it" (Matt. 16:25a). This life is not the ultimate. Following Jesus is.

There is *pain* but it will pass. There is *disappointment* but it will not last. There is *grief* but there is reuniting. There is *sacrifice* but there is reward. There is *loss* but there is gain.

Follow Christ when others disapprove. Follow Christ when others scorn. Follow Christ and discover the mystic self.

Lose Your Life

Lose the "muttness." Quit fretting over salary structures and pay raises. Stop picking at other staff members if their budget is larger. Lose your life. Hard words! Jesus did not encourage His disciples to take care of themselves at others' cost. He said, "whoever loses his life for me will find it" (Matt. 16:25b). Forget the small stuff.

It's impossible to plot revenge against someone who embarrassed you in the choir and lose your life for Christ at the same time. It's impossible!

Lose your life means pay attention to priorities, love your enemies, do good to those that use you, give others the benefit of the doubt, and let your life reflect Jesus so that the mystic in you is overpowering the mutt in you.

Note

1. Daniel Goleman, *Vital Lies, Simple Truths* (New York: Simon and Schuster, 1985), 102-04.

4

A Green Card for Goliath Frogs

"The man I meet is seldom as instructive as the silence he breaks."[1]

"Doubtless you are the people, and wisdom will die with you" (Job 12:2).

Recently, a group of people brought some Goliath frogs from Africa with the express purpose of entering them in a frog-jumping contest. They had experimented with steroids, and the frogs were ten times larger than the American frogs, which were common to ponds. These frogs were monstrous. Officials refused their entry. One said, "Too much hype!" Another said, "It takes away the fun of the sport."

Still, the Goliath-frog creators tried to get a green card for the frogs in order to make them American citizens (so to speak). At a later time they would enter them in frog-jumping contests or sell them in large quantities for Goliath frog-legs sales. They reasoned it would be a great idea for a chain of restaurants with options for expansion.

Goliath frogs in ministry may not be as strange as it seems. Some try ministerial steroids to become Goliath frogs.

The Steroids for Ministerial Goliath Frogs

The Language of Zion

"God told me to wear the brown suit instead of the blue one," one church member told another. She was serious. I was there.

Have you heard people say things like: "I have prayed about this, and it is God's will that we build this building. The 'spiritual' people will support me." "I know you have expressed your disapproval as a congregation of the two Sunday

Schools, but we have to do what God has told us to do." "This is the right person to lead our Christian education program. You can trust me. I have prayed about this."

Who could argue with those statements? Goliath frogs can get pumped up beyond normal size. The steroids of the language of Zion convince some.

Although Thoreau was cynical about ministers, we would do well to listen to him: "The man I meet is seldom as instructive as the silence he breaks."

Job was caught in the middle of a group of spiritual Goliath frogs searching for the green card of validation. Bildad, Eliphaz, Zophar, and Elihu were sharing their "binah" of understanding and intelligence.

"If you devote your heart to him and stretch out your hands to him, if you put away the sin that is in your hand and allow no evil to dwell in your tent, then you will lift up your face without shame. . . . Life will be brighter than noonday" (Job 11:13-15,17). Zophar was waxing eloquent. He was pumped with the steroids of spiritual advice.

Job responded, "doubtless you are the people and wisdom will die with you!" (Job 12:1-2). Job was saying, "You are a great religious talker, but you don't know the slightest thing about my pain." Jump, Frog, but not into my pond. Get away from me.

Accolades from Others

Any behaviorist worth his or her salt knows the value of affirmation. But, accolades can cloud good judgment unless filtered with love and good sense.

Some use accolades to get what they want—attention, affirmation, and approval for themselves. *Knowing when to digest accolades will build intestinal fortitude. Knowing when to discard accolades will avoid a stomach virus of spiritual steroids.*

Power

The devil knew the impact of power. He promised Jesus recognition and superiority. Jesus knew the trap. Some ministerial Goliath frogs don't. Television exposure and contributions can do much to distort morality. History has proven it during the past few years. "They can't touch me," said one television evangelist. He was wrong.

Power is so fleeting, so unpredictable. It has no place in the service of Christ. Goliath frogs want to be ten times larger than ordinary frogs. They want to be "greatest." The disciples had the same question: "Who is the greatest?" (Matt. 18:1*b*).

Jesus' response was, "Become like little children" (v. 3). Learn, grow, and enjoy innocence. You don't have to be parent to the world. You don't have to be in charge.

Power is not what it appears. Consider, you win the frog-jumping contest. What's next? A larger Goliath frog lurks in the shadows.

Consider, you have the largest church budget in town. Larger budgets mean larger responsibilities. Some churches will outgrow your budget. After you've had the largest, can you make the most of what you have? Or is the addiction to power so great that the perspective of the little child is lost?

Be careful what you ask for; you might get it. If it's power and you get it, then what?

How to Avoid the Temptation of Becoming a Goliath Frog

Job said, "You, however, smear me with lies; you are worthless physicians, all of you! If only you would be altogether silent! For you, that would be wisdom" (Job 13:4-5).

Larry Richards shares the Ann Landers story about a woman who had twelve miscarriages. She signed her letter as "Empty Cradle." One Goliath frog wrote to her: "Accept the fact that you weren't meant to have children and get your tubes tied."

Another simply said, "You must have miscounted."

Then there was the spiritual giant who said, "God is trying to tell you something."

"Empty Cradle" wrote: "Each miscarriage is more difficult. Every time it happens, I lose faith all over again."

Finally, she met a stranger who tried to make her feel better. The stranger in a store had a baby in a shopping cart. "Empty Cradle" went over and touched the baby's foot and began to cry. The stranger put her arm around her and the baby, and the three of them stood in the middle of the store for several seconds while "Empty Cradle" cried.

Only three words were spoken: "Are you OK?"

"Empty Cradle" responded, "I'm fine."[2] There is a message in this story.

Don't Try to Shoulder All of God's Work

We can't do all of God's work. He doesn't expect that. We can, however, do a little. God doesn't expect us to be spiritual giants. He doesn't need Goliath frogs. He needs us to be "appropriately compassionate." We should not press it, strain it, or exhaust it. We should be appropriately compassionate.

Most ministers cannot visit every church member in every hospital daily. There isn't time. All shut-ins cannot receive as much attention as they need or deserve. There isn't time. All committees cannot have the undivided attention of a minister. Again, time is a problem. Every lost person cannot be visited as often as one would like. There is a limit. A minister cannot do all of God's work. After all, it is God's work. He can handle it. Before we spread ourselves too thin, maybe we should give God room to spread His work to several, instead of the few.

Thoreau wrote,

> Whate'er we leave to God, God does,
> And blesses us;
> The work we choose should be our own
> God lets alone.[3]

God doesn't make puppets of us. He turns us loose to do His work. On the other hand, He doesn't expect us to be puppeteers—pulling the strings of others to get His work done. God is perfectly able to get His work done with many of His children. He does not need compulsive-obsessives trying to do all of His work for Him.

Be Careful What You Use to Get "Pumped"

A steroid-type drug in ministry might be, "It worked before in that church. Why not here?" We get "pumped" from others' successes. Of course, what works in one church may bomb in another.

Job's friends called attention to what had worked in the past. "Life will be brighter than noonday" (Job 11:17). All you have to do is what has been done. Devote your heart, stretch out your hands, and put away the sin.

All these pious platitudes to Job were based on assumptions. Job's "friends" assumed that he was out of synch with God's will. They thought: *Do what has been done before, and it'll all work out all right.* They were so sure of it that they spent days giving him advice. They knew they were right. They were "pumped" with self-assurance. However, they were wrong.

Winning and Losing Are Both Temporary

What's so great about winning a frog-jumping contest? What's so great about being the largest frog on the jumping block? What's so great about being the best, biggest, or baddest? It's only temporary.

Job responded to his friends: "Though he slay me, yet will I hope in him; I will surely defend my ways to his face. Indeed, *this will turn out for my deliverance"* (Job 13:15-16, author's italics).

At some risk of heresy it is my contention we are not in the business of Goliath-frog mentality in churches. We are not called to "best" others. We are in the business of being Christ's ambassadors of love and truth. We are only sinners, but we will be delivered. We may be ridiculed. At times we may look ridiculous. Others may judge us or jump farther. We, like Job, can defend our ways if we are faithful. This will *turn out for our deliverance.*

Conclusion

There is a Bildad, Eliphaz, Zophar, and Elihu in most every church. Hear their cries: "Why is that church growing faster than us? It must be because we have a less spiritual staff." "If you would just preach the Bible, we could grow faster than any church in our association or state." "Our music is just not meeting the needs of our people. It lacks something." "Our church used to run 400 in Sunday School. Now we do good to have 225. What's wrong with our minister of education?"

Job remained faithful! He knew his heart. He knew the hypocrisy and impatience of his friends. He longed for comfort and affirmation. Some are incapable of comfort and affirmation if the need to jump farther is greater than the need to comfort and affirm.

I never liked frogs. Frogs that are ten times larger than normal because of artificial means just give me more to dislike about them. They are ugly and slimy. They sing no songs of joy. They are unpredictable.

I have a suggestion. If we must Americanize Goliath frogs and give them a green card, then let's find a giant lily pad in the middle of a remote pond for them. Also, let's give them a small pond. That way, they can be what they desire—a big frog in a little pond. Let them live with the delusion of grandeur.

Notes

1. Henry David Thoreau, as quoted in *Christian Poetry,* comp. Pat Alexander (Grand Rapids: Wm. B. Eerdmans, 1981), 55.

2. Larry Richards, *When People You Trust Let You Down* (Waco, Tex.: Word, 1987), 89.

3. Thoreau, "Inspiration" in Alexander, 55.

5

An Omelet Is Several Broken Eggs

"Bear with each other and forgive whatever grievances you may have against one another" (Col. 3:13).

"Remember the tea kettle. Though up to its neck in hot water, it continues to sing."

"Make the best of it" sounds like great advice. The problem is there are times you just don't want advice.

Romans 8:28 is a wonderful passage of comfort. "And we know that in all things God works for the good of those who love him." But it sounds empty if a spouse is dying of cancer. It sounds flat if a fifteen-year-old daughter is pregnant outside of wedlock. It sounds repulsive if a son has AIDS. There are times it just doesn't feel like there is a "best."

Broken Eggs in Life

Anxiety

Anxiety is a feeling of uncertainty, sometimes panic. Often we know where anxiety originates. Frequently, we do not.

If the bank account is smaller than the bills, we are anxious. If a recurring pain cannot be easily diagnosed, we are anxious. If a friendly church member becomes suddenly distant, we are anxious. If a problem in church cannot be solved, we are anxious. If a disgruntled staff member is having frequent lunches with a prominent church leader, we are anxious.

There was a sign on a fence in the Indiana countryside which read: "If you cross this field you had better do it in 9.8 seconds. The bull can do it in 10 seconds. No Trespassing."[1] Now, that's anxiety.

Is there any staff member alive who has not seen that sign in his or her mind? Anxiety is a terrible thing.

Archibald Hart's book *Overcoming Anxiety* suggests some unhealthy ways people use to deal with anxiety.

Repression.—We try to put it out of our awareness. It is like paving an interstate without filling the pothole. It just won't work. The pothole is still there.

Denial.—It is a mental shield used to deflect a threat. A thin black plastic is laid over the pothole. Of course it will not hold the weight of an automobile.

Obsessions.—A notion that gets fixed or stuck in the mind becomes an obsession. Rigidity, inflexibility, and perfectionism are examples. The pothole is not there! Of course the hard reality is felt when the automobile is driven across the pothole.[2]

Broken Relationships

Paul encouraged the church members of Colossae to "forgive whatever grievances," but Paul did not stay long in one place. Being a missionary, he kept moving on to other churches. Just about the time the "honeymoon" was over, he changed churches.

A staff member may break some eggs with other staff members, but each still has to face the other on Monday morning at staff meeting. It is difficult to stay spiritual when words of unguarded candor have been spoken. The words of prayer are there. The spirit of prayer is difficult.

Once Buddy Hackett told a *Tonight Show* audience, "I've had arguments with people but I never carry a grudge. You know why I don't? While you're carrying a grudge, they're out dancing." Some people carry grudges that have forgotten beginnings. They waste all that energy with a forgotten reason.

The second time Paul wrote to the church at Thessalonica, he said, "the love every one of you has for each other is increasing" (2 Thess. 1:3*b*). That is how it should be.

Broken relationships are like broken eggs in another way: If something isn't done right away, the odor will become unbearable.

"Who's in Charge"

Recently a retired executive, who in reality was pushed aside to a staff position, was heard to say, "Last week I had fifty persons under me. This week I have no one."

Of course what he meant was he was no longer supervising persons who were "under" him in the organization. Perhaps his confession was more sardonic than sarcastic. He felt colleagues were "under" him. The "I'm-in-charge" mentality has done a great deal to break a lot of eggs.

The tip-off is usually subtle. *My staff* is a phrase most church staff members cringe at hearing from a pastor. One staff member responded, "I don't belong to him." Again, the subtle reminder is "I'm in charge." Team spirit is not a high priority.

All kinds of conjectures exist about why some need to be in charge.

- Insecurity—the unfulfilled need to be equal or superior.
- Obsessiveness—the compelling need to be and do with no fulfillment.
- Helplessness—the need to be respected but getting a "Rodney Dangerfield" feeling instead.

To me *why* doesn't seem as important as *how*. How we come across is extremely important. If a subliminal message of "I'm in charge" is communicated, a church staff will feel dumped on.

Broken Eggs Are Omelets

Herbert Hoover, in spite of dismal crises and failures during his presidency, was presented the Horatio Alger Award for effectiveness in leadership. When asked what the secret of his success was, he said, "With the help of God, I never gave up."[3]

"You take the hand you have been dealt in life," a paraplegic woman told me once. She was not maudlin. But how is it possible to turn broken eggs into omelets?

Go One More Round (Perserverance)

"Go one more round" is what Archie Moore said it took to be a champion.[4]

On Monday morning many of us feel we have fought the last round we can muster. By noon most of us have torn up our resignation and decided to go one more round. We are ready to make the omelet. (Forgive the mixed metaphors.)

> When things go wrong as they sometimes will,
> When the road you're trudging seems all uphill,
> When the funds are low and the debts are high,
> And you want to smile but you have to sigh,
> When care is pressing you down a bit,
> Rest if you must, but don't you quit.[5]

Something can be done with this crisis. It can be solved. In the roll call of faith, the writer of Hebrews said "none of them received what had been promised. God had planned something better for us so that only together with us would they be made perfect" (Heb. 11:39-40). The broken promises were temporary. It took the completion of the roll call of faith to make sense of those who had suffered previously in history. The faithful went one more round and destiny was the result. Jesus' mission was to give fulfillment to the law through grace. Grace was by faith. The faithful gave us the model. Go one more round than you think you can, and you will receive grace. Grace is for the faithful.

Paul told the Philippians, "Do not be anxious about anything" (Phil. 4:6). The opposite would be panic, hysteria, or worse yet to quit. Roberto Duran fought Sugar Ray Leonard for the welterweight championship of the world. In the eighth round, Duran quit. It was called the "no mas" (no more) fight and will live in infamy because Duran was so frustrated he felt he couldn't take anymore. He could not, or would not, go one more round. His anxiety overwhelmed him.

Pick Out the Eggshells (Precaution)

Not much can be done with eggshells. They must be cleaned out.

Paul said, "I have learned the secret of being content in any and every situation, whether well fed or hungry, whether living in plenty or in want" (Phil. 4:12b).

Take your time. Break the eggs gently. If you get eggshells in the pan, pick them out. Learn to deal with each situation.

Don't panic. Don't get hysterical. Expect some bad press. Your congregation is made up of human beings who will react strangely at times. Clean out the eggshells before you clean out your locker and resign.

The temptation is to throw out the eggs. Occasionally, they cannot be salvaged. Most of the time they can. So pick out the eggshells.

What are some of the eggshells?

- Guilt—particularly when "inordinate"
- Impatience
- Hurt feelings
- Impulsiveness
- Anxiety

Give It Your Best Shot (Maximum Effort)

"I can do everything through him who gives me strength" (Phil. 4:13).

I am not a great cook. I make homemade biscuits. When properly coached, I can even make an omelet. When my wife was recovering from heart surgery, I knew I had to take on the household chores. I cooked. I cleaned. I carried my weight. Occasionally, I carried my weight reluctantly, but I gave it my best shot, in spite of feeling pitiful.

Gymnast Cathy Rigby was a member of the 1972 Olympic team in Munich. She trained hard over a period of years. She did a good routine, but her name was not called when the winners were announced. She joined her parents for a good cry. As she sat down, she could barely manage to say, "I'm sorry. I did my best."

"You know that, and I know that," her mother said, "and I'm sure God knows that, too."

Then, Cathy recalls, her mother said ten words that she has never forgotten: Doing your best is more important than being the best.[6]

Cathy gave it her best shot. That's all anyone can expect. At least, that's all God expects.

Try to avoid breaking the eggs. If you break the eggs, make an omelet.

Notes

1. *Bits and Pieces* (Fairfield, N.J.: Economics Press, 1985), 24.
2. Archibald Hart, *Overcoming Anxiety* (Waco, Tex.: Word, 1989), 110-13.
3. Hardy R. Denham, Jr., *Living Toward a Vision* (Nashville: Broadman, 1980), 45.
4. Ibid., 46.
5. Ibid.
6. *Soundings* (Fairfield, N.J.: Economics Press, 1988), 1-2.

6

Bumper-Sticker Christians

"A gift becomes a gift only when it is accepted."[1]

"And what does the Lord require of you? To act justly and to love mercy and to walk humbly with your God" (Mic. 6:8).

"To one there is given through the Spirit the message of wisdom, to another the message of knowledge by means of the same Spirit, to another faith . . . healing . . . miraculous powers . . . prophecy" (1 Cor. 12:8-9).

Bumper stickers intrigue me. They communicate so much so quickly. They're memorable. These are some I've actually seen:

- Don't laugh, it's paid for.
- Baby on board.
- Mother-in-law in trunk.
- I'm not well. I'm not even getting better.
- I've been sick. Back off!
- Bleeaah!
- I'm the fat lady, but I don't sing. So it ain't over.
- One side of a bumper sticker said, "I'm a schizophrenic." The other side said, "No, I'm not."

I haven't seen these but I heard about them.

- I don't have egg on my face. I'm just yellow.
- Help! I'm Single!
- Draw! (I think he was an old-time gunfighter.)

We have bumper-sticker insignias in churches, too. They are not as visible, but they communicate clearly. Here are a few.

- You should hear our choir.
- Our pastor never puts us down.
- Our pastor always puts us down.
- Our youth program has something for everyone.
- Our youth program has little for anyone.
- Music is fantastic.
- Music is too high church.
- Music is too toe-tapping.
- Too friendly!
- Too unfriendly!
- Something for everyone.

Bumper-Sticker Witnessing Is a Means, Not an End

Bumper-sticker witnessing is a lot like a ten-second commercial on television for an automobile. It will not sell the automobile. It has, however, planted the seed. The shopping, looking, negotiating, and decision to buy is still to come. But a brief and memorable message about Christ has been left with a person who needs the gospel.

A first-visit witness is essential. It is a lot like the bumper-sticker mentality. But, the work has just begun. This is a *means* to sharing Christ with a person, not an *end*. Continued interest, telephone calls, follow-up visits, and involvement in church activities will come later.

I have often cringed at the statement: "I won John to the Lord." It sounds self-indulgent. What about parents, teachers, friends, and other conversations? Did these persons play no part? I would be happy to be one of the many instruments to lead someone to Christ. "I won" distorts the meaning, at least, to me. How much better to hear, "He accepted Christ as his personal Savior."

The psalmist said, "Pride is their necklace" (Ps. 73.6). Religious people wear the necklace, too—especially about witnessing.

Bumper-Stickers of Christians

Paul talked about the bumper stickers we wear in 1 Corinthians 12:8*ff.* Let's look a little closer at a few of them.

Wisdom

It is difficult to isolate characteristics of wisdom. Those who desire wisdom rarely have it. Those who have it rarely know it. However, it is there to see—like a bumper sticker.

One interpretation of wisdom is "deeper insight which can turn knowledge to the best advantage."[2]

Wisdom is timing. It is knowing *when* and *how*. Knowledge is knowing *what*. Intelligent people give information, sometimes indiscriminately. Wise people give information expediently, upon request. Intelligent people often speak from retention. Wise people speak from assimilated facts that are relevant. It is hard to know a wise person when you see one. After a period of time, he or she is unmistakable.

Few bumper stickers tell the good news of Christ as loudly as wisdom.

Knowledge

We need persons with 135 I.Q.'s Although threatening to some, they are important to making good decisions. Facts are essential. Those who do not know history will relive it, warts and all! Although we wish they would not wear this bumper sticker with such glee, nevertheless we need people with knowledge.

A theatrical celebrity was asked to quote Psalm 23. He did so with much applause.

An acquaintance of another guest, who was a minister, saw his opportunity. The acquaintance did not like the minister. With sarcasm he asked the minister to repeat the psalm thinking he would be upstaged by the theatrical celebrity. Reluctantly, the minister obliged. Upon completion, there was no applause—neither was there a dry eye in the house.

The confused acquaintance asked the celebrity, "What was the difference? You were wonderful, but he seemed to touch the audience on a different level."

"The difference is simple," said the celebrity. "I know the psalm. He knows the Shepherd."

We must have those with the gift of knowledge. We must, also, have those with wisdom. Both are the utterance of the same Spirit.

Faith

This is contagious faith. It is the kind of faith that others seek out. When the conditions are most adverse, people with this bumper sticker are sought. They have an intangible quality of trust. Their smile is not plastic. It has no shades of hypocrisy. It is real and genuine.

This faith is best when others are at their worst. It is the childlike, naive feeling that others watch, observe, and admire. They wish they had it.

Healing

Jesus' message was for the whole person. Pain is not an illusion. It is an indication that something is wrong. It should be remedied.

The gift of healing has taken on new significance in this century. The gift of pastoral care and counseling is not a bumper sticker all Christians can wear, but some can. The progress clinical pastoral education has made in this century has been remarkable. Anton Boisen, Harry Stack Sullivan, Wayne Oates, C. W. Brister, H. J. M. Nouwen, D. K. Switzer, and Scott Peck are just a few that have changed our thinking about the remarkable gift of healing.

Unfortunately many still hold that the "spontaneous" and "instantaneous" visual or verbal transformation is the *only* kind of healing. Charlatans have gotten rich making others believe this farce.

Healing is often slow. The redemption process is instantaneous. The growing in Christ process is not so instantaneous. Healing is not a cheap sideshow. It is not for the purpose of making a man look untouchable but for God's glory. Consequently, it is often slow.

Recovery of sight is no longer foreign to functional blindness, but it is the result of the gift of healing. Movement is no longer foreign to functional paralysis, but it is the result of the gift of healing. It is miraculous healing. The restoration of a healthy mind is no longer foreign to a disturbed person but it is still miraculous healing. All healing is divine. A less dramatic time period does not make it less divine.

Prophecy

Prophecy is interpreting what will be on the basis of what is. *Prophecy* is understanding the trends of events. The Old Testament is a wonderful compilation of prophets.

We still have prophets. Those who proclaim themselves to be prophets rarely are. These persons often "predict." A real prophet "forewarns."

A practical characteristic of a prophet is skill for planning. A prophet looks at trends in Sunday School, discipleship, worship, and missions and leads a church to plan for the future. It doesn't sound so dramatically spiritual, but it is a vital skill for a church about to build.

There are others—miracles, discernment, tongues, and interpretation. Bumper stickers tell about a part of us, but not all.

Conclusion

I want my bumper sticker to read, "Although a sinner, God loves me anyway." (Thank you, Will Campbell, for the idea.)

I don't want to hide my humanity. Neither do I want to display my sinful nature. God loves me. Even though I am human, He loves me. Even though I am sinful, He loves me. He doesn't want me to be sinful, but He loves me.

How do you want your bumper sticker to read?

Notes

1. Henri J. M. Nouwen, *With Open Hands* (Notre Dame, Ind.: Ava Maria Press, 1974), 62.

2. *The Interpreter's Bible*, vol. 10 (New York: Abingdon Press, 1953), 151.

7

Distractions

"But Martha was distracted by all the preparations"
(Luke 10:40).

"It's not like you could put it on and just go strolling
somewhere. I don't know what anybody would do with it."[1]

You would think people would think before they act. However, some don't.
Many are distracted with secondary issues and neglect the primary issues.

In psychology circles, people who are overly distracted by secondary issues are
called *compulsive obsessives*. They work as hard on the distractions as they do on
the primary objects. These persons apparently can't help themselves.

A man who had been a compulsive obsessive in life had driven his wife crazy.
He worked fourteen-hour days. He brought his work home with him. He complained about the cleanliness of the house, the proper time for meals, the children's education, and the wife's personal habits. He never stopped.

He died. The woman had her husband cremated. She put the ashes in an hour-
glass. Each time she walked by, she turned him upside down and said, "Work you
rascal, you, work!" (Thank you, Paul Powell for that one.)

Martha's Secondary Issues

It is easy to get distracted with secondary issues.

Martha Wanted to Make a Perfectionistic Impression

A compulsive obsessive wants others to know it. It is true Martha opened her
home to Jesus. He was a celebrity, a religious celebrity. He was known in the
village before He arrived. Martha wanted to "cash in" on the notoriety.

Additionally, she was a warm person. When you put together compassion and
obsession, you frequently get compulsive action. Some religious people volunteer

for more than they are able to do. They like the pastor. They like the minister of music. They want them to know that they are religious. The pastor is a visible person. One way to get his attention is to be too involved in activities. It is not unusual for these persons to neglect their families to attend committee meetings at the church. The committee meetings are important. The family is more important.

It is not unusual for those who want to make an impression to be perfectionists. You have heard their battle cry, *If you can't do it right, don't do it.* It has been a tape played in their mind for decades.

Some characteristics of perfectionism are:

Dichotomous thinking.—This means "all or none." There is no gray. There is only success or failure. There is no in between. There is no room for compromise.

The positive thing about dichotomous thinking is that it is not ambivalent. There is no in between. Unlike the story told in seminary about one of my professors. (In truth, it may be apocryphal.)

A student challenged the ambivalence of a professor who appeared to straddle the fence on a particularly sensitive theological issue. "I have heard that you can speak as eloquently on one side of this issue as you can the other. Is that true?" the student asked.

The professor replied, "Well, yes and no!"

Dichotomous thinking does not allow the phrase, "I don't know."

Rigidity.—This may be a first cousin of dichotomous thinking. But, rigidity adds another dimension. Rigid people seem to depend on unswerving opinions for their own self-esteem.

"I want" becomes "I need." "I must" can be felt in the pleas of a minister who wants to sell his or her ideas without possibility of differing opinions.

A group of ministers of education were gathered in a seminar on "Success in Ministry." These persons had mutually agreed it is almost impossible to "succeed" in their work without the support of the pastor. In the course of conversation, one person said, "Once our pastor makes up his mind, you can't budge him." It was meant as a compliment. However, you could feel the resistance in the statement. Few persons enjoy being around someone who will not budge once he or she has made up his or her mind. These are rigid persons.

The hurdle factor.—Perfectionists are so focused on the hurdles ahead that there is little appreciation of the hurdles already cleared. *Martha* concentrated on a clean house, clean dishes, and social protocol. She wanted to be sure that the meal included a green vegetable, a white vegetable, a proper salad fork, multiple choices of salad dressing, and only one meat, properly cooked. OK, OK, so they weren't that nutritionally conscious! But, she was *focused*. The fact that Jesus had come to her house was secondary to making the right impression. Perfectionists are always looking ahead, and it is difficult for them to appreciate the wins.

Telescoping.—The focus of what a perfectionist wants to do is clear and clean. The problem is that they often have poor peripheral vision.

In relationships, a perfectionist knows there is a serious problem only when it is too late. A wife may focus so desperately on a clean house that she forgets to welcome her husband with affection. A child may focus so hard on making and keeping friends that he forgets that the primary nourishment for his growth is his family.

Martha Was a Tattletale

"Lord, don't you care that my sister has left me to do the work by myself? Tell her to help me!" (Luke 10:40).

Have you noticed that persons who get distracted easily want to blame others when things fall apart. "It's not my fault the supper's late. Mary is the one on the floor."

When all else fails, blame someone. "I don't do windows," said a distraught minister of music who was asked to participate in the church visitation. "I have the work of the music organization to care for. Why is our minister of education always picking on me, anyway?" he may ask. You could almost hear the refrain, "Make him stop, Pastor." People who get distracted are often tattletales.

Mary Chose What Was Better

"You are worried and upset about many things, but only one thing is needed. Mary has chosen what is better, and it will not be taken away from her" (v. 41).

In the statement from *Newsweek* at the beginning of this devotional, one wonders what a person would do with an $8,200 parrot costume. The idea of having a souvenir may be intriguing. However, to whom are you going to show it? The thief could have made a better choice, but distractions do that to you. You get preoccupied with what looks good and forget what is better.

Some people find a Bach chorale inspiring. But a Gaither chorus inspires others. Knowing what is appropriate is better than "doing what is best for others." A staff member must consider the needs of the congregation. Like Mary, we should choose what is better.

Some Lessons Martha Should Take from Mary

Martha could learn a lot from Mary. Distracted people can learn from people who put Christ first in their lives.

Celebrate the Victories

A coach and his team had just won an improbable victory. The reporter asked him, "Well, you play L.S.U. on Monday, will you be ready?" "Hey," the coach replied, "let me savor the victory. It's only been ten minutes."

A church has a high-attendance record. The conscientious minister of education announces the record, but then adds, "But what are we going to do next Sunday?"

Celebrate the victories.

Learn to Live with Imperfection

Some things aren't worth doing perfectly. The house may not be immaculate, but Jesus is there. Stop puttering. Stop looking for things to do to get ready. There is nothing to get ready for. He is here.

Lower Your Expectations

Martha, you don't have to be the best housekeeper and cook in the world. Stop and smell the roses. Stop and listen. That is what Mary did. She stopped and listened. That is a great compliment.

Lower your expectations of Mary. Lower your expectations of yourself.

Look for Spontaneity

Spontaneous people are fun to be around. They seize the moment. They are intrigued with what is happening. Distracted people do not see what is going on around them because they are so focused.

One woman told her friend, "I don't know why I love my husband so much after twenty-five years. Perhaps it's because he makes me laugh. He is always full of surprises and definitely unpredictable. Hey, I might just have told you three reasons why I love him."

Look for spontaneity. "Only one thing is needed," Jesus told Martha. Give your attention to the proper things in life, and the secondary things will not distract you.

Note

1. This was Pittsburgh Pirates spokesman Rick Cerrone's comment on the new $8,200 parrot costume stolen from the mascot's car. *Newsweek,* February 12, 1990, 17.

8

A *Titanic* or a *Valdez?*

"Whoever flees from the terror will fall into the pit, And the one who climbs up out of the pit will be caught in the snare" (Jer. 48:44).

"There is no man so good, who, were he to submit all his thoughts and actions to the laws would not deserve hanging ten times in his life."—Michel de Montaigne

"If the ship goes down, are the lifeboats safe?"

We were on the Emerald Seas and having an emergency drill on deck. My wife, Shirley, said, "If this ship goes down, are these lifeboats safe?" Good question!

Jeremiah's Ministry

Jeremiah's ministry spanned forty years— from 625 B.C. to 586 B.C. Manasseh ruled during fifty years of religious apostasy. Josiah followed with religious reform (621-607); Jeremiah supported Josiah. But, he realized the people's hearts were not being changed. The battle of Carchemish (605 B.C.) established the Babylonian control over western Asia. Jeremiah preached submission to Babylon.

In the first part of Jeremiah we see the conditions of the times (chs. 7-13). The second part shows Jeremiah's relationship to God (chs. 14-33). Jeremiah then became God's *warrior* and *witness* (chs. 34-52).

In Jeremiah 48:44, we see a strange verse in the prophecy against Moab, "The one who flees from the terror will fall into the pit, And the one who climbs up out of the pit will be caught in the snare."

Two tragic sea events are a parallel. On the one hand is the *Titanic*. On the night of April 14-15, 1912, during its first trip from England to New York City it struck an iceberg and sank. It was 1,600 miles northeast of New York City; 2,200 persons were on board. Only 705 survived. The *Carpathia* picked up the survivors. The *Titanic* was the largest ship in the world, 882.5 feet long—twice as long as Noah's ark.[1]

In 1989, the Exxon *Valdez* spilled millions of gallons of oil after running aground. It affected hundreds of miles of seashore in Alaska, killing fish and wildlife. Dozens of lawsuits have already been filed.

One incident was a tragedy of lost lives. The other was a tragedy of disgrace and environmental hazard. Both affected world affairs.

The bottom line is: you can't lift yourself out of the sea of depravity by your own bootstraps. You must have help. The sea is too deep. There are too many obstacles.

Michel de Montaigne wrote, "There is no man so good, who, were he to submit all his thoughts and actions to the laws would not deserve hanging ten times in his life."[2]

The Minnesota Crime Commission released this statement,

> Every baby starts his life as a little savage. He is completely selfish and self-centered. He wants what he wants when he wants it—his bottle, his mother's attention, his playmate's toy, his uncle's watch. Deny him these once, and he seethes with rage and aggressiveness, which would be murderous were he not so helpless. He is in fact, dirty. He has no morals, no knowledge, no skills. Children are born delinquent. If permitted to continue in the self-centered world of his infancy . . . every child would grow up a criminal.[3]

Wayne Oates told a conference at Cedarmore, Kentucky, in April 1989 that he had a physician friend who had a new baby. She said, "He is totally self-centered. He has a ravenous uncontrollable appetite at one end and a total lack of responsibility at the other."

You can't lift yourself out of the sea of depravity by your own bootstraps. Not even the *Carpathia* will always be there. There are parents to guide babies. God will love us into discipline if we let Him. Paul tells us "There is no one righteous, not even one. There is no one who understands" (Rom. 3:10). Later, "For all have sinned and fall short of the glory of God" (v. 23).

We may get off the *Titanic* onto the *Carpathia* only to find the *Carpathia* is the Exxon *Valdez*. That would be tragic if it were the end of the story, but it is not. Man is depraved, but God is able. There is tragedy, but there is retribution. There is crisis, but there is hope.

At the beginning, the word of the Lord came to Jeremiah, "Before I formed you in the womb, I knew you, and before you were born I consecrated you" (Jer. 1:5, NASB). Later, " 'And they will fight against you, but they will not overcome you, for I am with you to deliver you,' declares the Lord" (v. 19, NASB).

Jeremiah learned how to cope. He felt the Babylonian captivity might make repentant citizens of Israel. When it did not change their hearts, he prophesied the downfall of Babylon. He adjusted. He coped. Ultimately, he loved his nation.

"My people have become lost sheep" (50:6, NASB). They have gone down with the *Titanic*. They have polluted the seas and animals with their depravity. "Their Redeemer is strong, the Lord of hosts is His name; He will vigorously plead their case, so that He may bring rest to the earth" (v. 34, NASB).

Lessons to Learn

There are some present-day lessons to be learned from the *Titanic* and the Exxon *Valdez*. Jeremiah will help us.

God Allows Us Freedom or Stupidity

The scariest part of life is that we are free. Nature is free to form icebergs. People are free to learn to cope. God allows freedom.

Natural resources like oil are God's creation. People are free to handle them responsibly *or not*. "It is He who made the earth by His power" (51:15, NASB). Later, "all mankind is stupid, devoid of knowledge" (v. 17, NASB). People have handled responsibly what God created.

God Expects Responsible Behavior

"Each of you save yourselves" (v. 45, NASB). Act responsibly. You can't pull yourself out of the sea of depravity by your own bootstraps. If you're in the water, you can take off your boots so you can swim.

The child allowed to continue in the self-centered world of his infancy will grow up to be a criminal. The love of the parent will not allow it. Acting responsibly is essential. Teaching responsibility to those we love is our ultimate obligation. God expects us to take control of the lies He has created for us. He expects us to be responsible.

God Is Able to Deal with Adversity

"For the Lord is a God of recompense, He will fully repay" (v. 56, NASB). *God can deal with scandal.*—A church that is emotionally and spiritually devastated can recover. The Lord is a God of recompense.

God can deal with disappointment.—A minister who was interviewed and considered for a position in a large church with a substantial salary increase was turned down. He was rejected. He devoted his energies to the church he was serving. God can deal with disappointment. The Lord is a God of recompense.

God can deal with grief.—A fifty-four-year-old woman lost her husband of thirty years. After two years of grief, she began to put her life back together. She began to get out. She devoted her life more to her church and made new friends—not easily, but with determination. The Lord is a God of recompense.

God can deal with culture shock.—A minister in a small rural church was called to an established suburban church with a measurably higher economic level. He was called a "hick" and an "incompetent." He adjusted. The church adjusted. He has now been there twenty-one years. The church is three times larger than when he came. He is loved by most. The Lord is a God of recompense and able to deal with adversity.

God Will Make the Unruly Uncomfortable

It is bad to have just enough religion to be miserable. It is God's work that creates conscience in decent people. "For the Lord is a God of recompense."

God Will Make the Righteous Have Peace

Even in the midst of the worst, Jeremiah found hope that God would take care of His own. "Before you were born I consecrated you" (1:5, NASB). Depravity is the condition of all men. God's grace is the solution to all depravity.

Notes

1. *The World Book Encylopedia,* vol. 19 (Chicago: Field Enterprises, 1972), 235.

2. Michel de Montaigne, *Quote Unquote,* ed. Lloyd Cory (Wheaton, Ill.: Victor Books, 1977), 297.

3. J. Dwight Pentecost, *Things Which Become Sound Doctrine* (Westwood, N.J.: Fleming H. Revell Co., 1965), 17-18.

9

The Can-Do People

"With my God I can scale a wall" (Ps. 18:29).

"A man at war with himself cannot be at peace with anyone."—Dag Hammersjold

Negative People

There may be only two kinds of people in the world—first, those who think they *can* and second, those who think they *can't*. This devotional is about the first type. First, a word about the second. Hopefully it will help us elevate the first.

Why do some persons see themselves as losers, failures, or can't people? Harriet Braiker writes about it in the December 1989 issue of *Psychology Today* about self talk.[1] She contends it is like tapes we begin to play to ourselves that help us either succeed or fail. Cheerful people play tapes that say you can do it. The second kind play tapes that say they can't.

David D. Burns explains some traps "negative-can't" people fall into.[2]

All or Nothing Thinking

Anything less than perfect is a failure. You can't be cheerful with that trap.

Overgeneralization

A single event reflects every event. If it's unpleasant, it's miserable and develops a pattern.

Mental Filter

One negative detail erases all praise. Recently, a person who had been rather heavy and had lost considerable weight was given a compliment. A colleague said, in the presence of several other colleagues, "You look great!"

For a couple of minutes this person was livid. Both were embarrassed. "I am sick and tired of being told how ugly I used to be." It was an embarrassing scene. The "mental filter" had activated. If we see ourselves as heavy, we filter out compliments.

Jumping to Negative Conclusions

Two variations are "mind reading" (someone is reacting negatively to you) and "fortune telling" (predictions that things will turn out badly). These persons discount the positive.

Magnification

Some people either minimize desirable qualities or exaggerate shortcomings. This is also called the "binocular" trick.

Emotional Reasoning

This is an assumption that feelings reflect the way things really are. (Such as: "I feel guilty. I must be a rotten person.")

"Should" Statements

Things should be the way you hoped or expected them to be.

A pastor called me and said, "I should be pastor of a substantial church at my age. I've been in the ministry eighteen years. What's wrong with me?"

"Maybe you're just a loser! Maybe you should just concede that fact and live miserably. You have a right to be miserable! What do you think?" I asked.

He laughed. He was a close friend. Later he told me he had really been thinking that way and my hassling him helped jolt him back to some clear thinking. It was a risk. I wouldn't recommend it. But, for a friend you care about sometimes gentle nudging is therapeutic.

Labeling

"I'm a loser." "I get no respect." This is the Rodney Dangerfield approach. Some do not get that way for comedy. It is tragedy. It's a great way to put yourself down and not have to contend with responsibility.

Uncheerful people like to play the game of Rodney Dangerfield. There is no risk of getting hurt or being rejected.

Blame

If San Francisco has an earthquake, somehow it is your fault. If a thirty-year-old daughter gets hooked on crack, it is your fault for failing as a parent. If a church is in decline, you're to blame. If a spouse is unhappy, you're to blame. If an eight-year-old son does not get on the Little League team, or a spouse gets sick, or your job is deleted, or the Berlin Wall goes back up, you're to blame.[3] "A man at war with himself cannot be at peace with anyone."

What Is A Cheerful "Liver?"

"With your help I *can* advance against a troop; with my God I *can* scale a wall" (Ps. 18:29, author's italics). The key word is *can!* Here are some tips for cheerful livers.

Know Your Limitations

Clint Eastwood said it in a *Dirty Harry* movie. It was not new. There are some things you can't do. That's all right. Know what you can do . . . with God's help.

Lean on Your Support System

"They confronted me in the day of my disaster, but the Lord was my support" (v. 18). God has emissaries. Your friends, spouse, children, and parents but also your church. God uses them all to give support.

Don't Lose Your Vision

God has a purpose for you. He has a mission for you. Cheerful livers know it and feel it. "O Lord, keep my lamp burning; my God turns my darkness into light" (v. 28).

Things get dim when you lose your vision about your mission.

"Is this what I'm supposed to be doing with my life?" may be a trap. A frustrating situation in a church may cloud your vision about your life. Refresh your memory. Recall your "call" to ministry. God has always had a plan. You are a part of it wherever you are. The ultimate purpose of God does not neglect your own individual contribution. God loves you. Don't lose your vision. "As for God, his way is perfect" (v. 30).

Keep Your Balance

Basketball has been fun for me. Unfortunately, I am "injury prone." About once every three months I lose my balance and suffer an injury. If I can disguise it from my wife, I do. She has little sympathy. After all, a fifty-four-year-old man should not be playing basketball, she reasons. It is essential for me to keep my balance and not suffer humiliation when I go home.

To be a cheerful liver you have to keep your balance. That wonderful verse in Psalm 18:36 reads, *"You broaden the path beneath me so that my ankles do not turn"* (author's italics). A narrow path is conducive to a sprained ankle. When four persons six to eight inches taller than I go for a rebound, the path is narrow. I should stand still and keep my balance. Most of the time I do. Sometimes I lose my head and don't. Then I am much more injury prone.

You have to keep your balance when activities around you are moving faster than your mind and body will let you move. A disgruntled church member, a new innovation in the educational program, a new minister of music trying innovative worship ideas, and a critical missions director simultaneously become vocal giving migraines to everyone on the staff. This is not the time to go for a rebound. This is not the time to "talk things out" with another staff member who has been "talked out" by the confusion. This is the time to keep your balance so you don't get your theological or emotional ankles turned.

Criticism Is Not Fatal

Cheerful livers know it. "Sticks and stones . . ." "You have delivered me from the attacks of the people" (v. 43). The psalmist knew it. David sang about it. Staff members must practice it. Criticism hurts! It is not fatal!

It comes with the territory. Visible leaders must contend with it. "A tender heart must be accompanied by a tough mind," Martin Luther King, Jr., told a group of students at The Southern Baptist Theological Seminary in 1960. He was right.

Some Things Are Temporary; Some Things Are Permanent

"The Lord lives! Praise be to my Rock!" (v. 46). Love is permanent. Articulate skills are temporary. Prophecy, wisdom, and even faith are temporary. Love is permanent. Benevolent giving, even pastoral care, is temporary. Love is permanent.

"He shows unfailing kindness to his anointed" (v. 50). That is the final verse in the song of Psalm 18. It is permanent. Love is permanent. God's love for us . . . our love to God . . . our love to others. It is permanent. Cheerful livers love!

Notes

1. Harriet Braiker, "The Power of Self Talk," *Psychology Today,* December 1989, 23.
2. David D. Burns, *The Good Feeling Handbook* (New York: William Morrow and Co., 1989).
3. Braiker, 24.

10

Squeeze the Turnip

"We are afflicted in every way but not crushed" (2 Cor. 4:8, NASB).

"We are hard pressed on every side, but not crushed" (2 Cor. 4:8).

"You can't get blood out of a turnip."

A racehorse was winding down in his competitive spirit. The jockey thought he could get one more good race. The racehorse was not sure. He told the racehorse, "Win today or its the milk wagon, tomorrow."

In less than 100 yards he was two furlongs behind. The jockey chided, ". . . milkwagon tomorrow." Within a half mile he was six furlongs behind the last thoroughbred. The irate jockey used his whip emphatically.

The racehorse, quite chagrined, turned and said, "Go easy on the whip. I gotta get up early in the morning."

There's just so much a person can do, then we have to face reality. There's just so much a person can take, then you live with total exasperation. Many of us live with total exasperation, and we live miserably.

Thus, we have the statement: "You can't get blood out of a turnip." It means . . . Don't expect me to be pleasant after nine hours with the kids. You can't get blood out of a turnip. Don't expect me to be pleasant after nine hours with my boss. You can't get blood out of a turnip.

I paid the doctor, grocer, the pharmacist, and Mastercard. Where will I get money for the Visa and Sears payment? You can't get blood . . .

My church reached an additional 10 percent in Sunday School enrollment within the last year. Last Sunday the chairman of deacons said our church was not reaching people.

The second letter of Paul to the church at Corinth was one of encouragement. The church had been disrupted with frivolous doctrine and scathing diversions. Now healing was important. A person with whom Paul strongly disagreed was embarrassed (2 Cor. 2:5*f*). Paul felt he had been punished enough. He was thought to be involved in an incestuous relationship, if that were the case, he had much to be forgiven for.[1]

Paul himself was being criticized. "He has no letter of recommendation" (see 3:1). "He is fickle" (1:15). "His preaching is weak" (4:3). "He is timid or bold at untimely times" (10:1). "He has no right to preach" (10:7).

No wonder Paul was writing "You can't get blood out of a turnip." I've been there. I don't want to be there again, although I probably will.

Paul's Four Crises

Paul faced four crises. None brought him to defeat. *The turnip lives.* Squeeze it.

Hemmed in but Not Crushed

Every way I turn there is more trouble. I'm living proof of Murphy's Law. (2 Cor. 4:8).

He was not crushed. The literal translation of this word is "straightened" *(stenochoromenoi)*.[2] Another way of looking at this is "Run over by a big truck but not 'flattened.'"

When you're hemmed in and the door is locked, it's time to cut out a window. If the unjust criticism keeps coming, get out of the office. Leave. Avoid the temptation to retaliate.

Helpless but Not Hopeless

"Perplexed but not in despair" (v. 8). In the Greek language it is a word play— *aporoumenoi* but not *exaporoumenoi*. The prefix *ex* means there is still a way out. I can't see it, but there is one. The one in despair says, "I can't see it therefore it isn't there."

I may be tied up, but if I keep wriggling, the ropes will loosen. I have made an error in judgment, but I can overcome it with responsibility.

A passenger in an airplane that made an emergency landing told an ABC newsman, "I had no control, but I had confidence in the pilot's skills. It was scary, but I never lost hope." Helpless but not hopeless.

Retreat—It's Not a Cop-Out

"Persecuted but not forsaken" (v. 9). It is literally translated *pursued* as in *retreat* from the field of battle. Sometimes you have to eat crow. It doesn't digest well, but you live.

The courage demanded in retreat is that it may be interpreted as cowardice. Turn away before alienating words are said. How many families could have been saved if this advice were heeded?

There is a time to walk away. There is a time to let another have his or her say. It may be humiliating, but it is not fatal. Eating crow will give indigestion, but it is not poisonous.

When the novelist-philosopher Dostoevski was imprisoned in solitary confinement because of his political opinions, every evening a soft, mysterious voice from another cell would say, "Courage brother, we also suffer." Suffering is a part of retreat. It is a bitter pill, but it puts things in perspective. We will survive to propagate the gospel of Christ.

Wounded but Not Fatally

"Struck down but not destroyed" (v. 9). This is a military phrase for having been hurt in battle. It hurts, but one will survive.

Paul was not just hurt physically; he was hurt in the heart. He was heart sick. I have been wounded in the battle of hearts. Someone may insult me, and I bleed, but I refuse to die.

It hurts more for a staff member to criticize us than it does for another church member to do so. Paul was hurt by the church at Corinth. These people worked alongside him in getting the church started. The people who were aiming the criticisms were staff persons—other ministers. Now they were taking aim at Paul. The term for *struck down* was not chosen lightly. It had been given thought. Paul was wounded, but he was not killed.

Some of the finest Christian people have been terminated from churches. They have survived, not easily, but they have survived.

Conclusion

You can squeeze a turnip but you can't get blood out of it. You can't get life out of it. You can't get a substance out of it that is not there. With Christ in us we have the substance to withstand any kind of adversity. Go ahead world, squeeze. We will survive. We have the same "spirit of faith" (v. 13) that has taken us through other adversity.

Notes

1. *The Broadman Bible Commentary,* vol. 2 (Nashville: Broadman, 1971), 2. See also 1 Cor. 5:1*ff.*

2. *The Interpreter's Bible,* vol. 10 (Nashville: Abingdon, 1953), 319.

11

From the Frying Pan into the Fire

"We do not need to defend ourselves before you in this matter. If we are thrown into the blazing furnace, the God we serve is able to save us from it, and he will rescue us from your hand, O king. But even if he does not, we want you to know, O king, that we will not serve your gods or worship the image of gold you have set up" (Dan. 3:16-18).

"From the frying pan into the fire."[1]

Gamblers call it the "hold card." Without a hold card you go from the frying pan into the fire. If you talk for a living, you learn the importance of listening. Listening shows respect. Listening is the hold card. Those who won't listen go from the frying pan into the fire.

A man was having a particularly difficult time in the hospital. He was old. He thought they had taken advantage of him. His wife was caring for him. A combination of drugs, old age, and weariness took their toll.

He said, "I want you to get out and not come back." He didn't mean it. She knew it. She was laughing as she told me.

"It was like jumping from the frying pan into the fire," she laughed. "I can't win." She loved him anyway. I admired her tough-mindedness.

A man many people admired, but many others disliked, had a wife with a debilitating disease. I was one that admired him. Each evening he went home and massaged her body from head to toe while she called him everything under the sun because of her pain. Later at work he was accused of an immoral act. He went home to face a lifeless body whose tongue worked just fine. In a more honest and unguarded moment, he said, "Every day I go from the frying pan into the fire."

Paul said, "For when I am weak, then I am strong" (2 Cor. 12:10).

Richard Bach was refused eighteen times before a publisher took a chance on *Jonathan Livingston Seagull*. Each time the refusal made him think he was facing another fire after being in a frying pan.

Golfers who practice frequently have a hold card. They are ready for recovery after a poor shot. Golfers who cheat have none. They will eventually get caught. Reality in golf is when you play with someone who really knows what you are scoring and counts your strokes. A cheater can't bear it. One who practices can.

Shadrach, Meshach, and Abednego held a "hold card." "Even if he does not [deliver them out of the furnace], we want you to know, O king, that we will not serve your gods or worship the image of gold you have set up" (Dan. 3:18). Their faith was their "hold card."

The real fury of Nebuchadnezzar was because Shadrach, Meshach, and Abednego paid no attention to Nebuchadnezzar's demand to serve his gods. He was mad. How mad was he? Mad enough to throw them into a blazing furnace.

Is there anything more infuriating than being ignored? When we go to coffee break we *talk,* all of us at the same time. No one listens. We like each other and function like family. Families compete for air time. Also, we are talkers by profession. All of us have ministerial mind-sets. It is easy to get left out. It is a matter of fact that not everyone will be heard. It's acceptable to be ignored by family. We expect it. Occasionally, it is even fun to see what can be done to be heard.

However, with strangers or persons we do not know well to be *ignored* is disconcerting. The astrologers were tattletales. They observed who was not worshiping the image of gold that had been set up by Nebuchadnezzar. The Jewish people were under siege. They had been appointed over the affairs of the province of Babylon. Shadrach, Meshach, and Abednego were not doing what they were supposed to be doing. They worshiped God.

Shadrach, Meshach, and Abednego were certain that God would deliver them out of the furnace. However, just in case, their "hold card" was their determination to worship God, even if God did not deliver them. "Even if he does not, . . . we will not serve your gods." They were willing to die.

So Nebuchadnezzar heated up the furnace . . . *seven times hotter* than usual. He tied up Shadrach, Meshach, and Abednego. Then he threw them into the furnace. The flames were so hot that they killed the soldiers who threw them into the furnace, but a strange thing happened. The three became four. That was strange, but they were also unbound and unharmed. That was even more strange.

The fourth person in the furnace looked like "a son of the gods" (v. 25). Old Testament scholars have had a field day interpreting this passage. Some say the phrase represents a Babylonian deity. Some suggest the Ugaritic texts suggest a Canaanite parallel.[2] The meaning is singularly apparent. This was an angel of God. The messianic implication is that Christ was *preincarnate.* Christ, who has always been eternal, was incarnate even before His birth.

When Nebuchadnezzar saw what had happened, he did an about-face. He had always made threats. Now, Nebuchadnezzar decreed, anyone who spoke against the God of Shadrach, Meshach, and Abednego would be "cut in pieces, and their houses shall be made a dunghill" (v. 29, KJV). Nebuchadnezzar had made a 360-degree turn in loyalty, but his technique remained the same. Kill them if they do not obey.

Paul once told Timothy, "Stir up the gift of God, which is in thee" (2 Tim. 1:6, KJV). Sometimes it takes adverse conditions to stir up the gift. Shadrach, Meshach, and Abednego were in adverse conditions. They reached deep within to find the gift. That was their "bird in the hand." They already had it. Their faith was already within. Paul continued, "God hath not given us the spirit of fear; but of power, and of love, and of a sound mind" (2 Tim. 1:7, KJV).

We may never face a blazing furnace, but we need the same ingredients of faith possessed by Shadrach, Meshach, and Abednego.

The Ingredients

Hope

They had hope—a vision to see what would become of them.—"We will not serve your gods" (Dan. 3:18). God would deliver them, but even if he did not, they had the vision of their determination to have faith in God.

There is comfort in a vision, but as Proverbs 29:18 says, "Where there is no vision the people perish."

Courage

They had determination to act out their vision in the face of great risk.—R. G. Lee once preached, "Anything *conceivable* and *believable* is *achievable* if you have faith in God." The zest for living is seen best in those who act out their vision. A church without a vision is pitiable, but a church with a vision will live forever.

Churches who act on their vision will face obstacles, but the risks are worth it. The conflict will eventually be resolved.

George Bernard Shaw was said to be a cynic. When discussing a person who was without vision, he said, "He died at 30; but was buried at 60." We must all act on our vision.

Before 1954 no one ran the mile in less than four minutes, now hundreds have done it. There was a mental barrier. The body has been stretched to endure more than the track experts thought it could. A vision of what can be done must be clear in our minds. If done properly, we set standards for hundreds of others.

Works

Actions speak louder than words.—Marshall McLuhan said, "After all has been said and done, more will have been said than done." Not so with Shadrach, Meshach, and Abednego. Their actions laid a tradition that spanned twenty-six centuries. It was a brief moment in biblical history, but their actions spoke louder than words.

A ship in the dock is safe, but ships are for traveling in water. Words are like a docked ship, but actions help us get over the troubled waters of living. Actions speak louder than words.

Commitment

Believe in Someone bigger than yourself.—Looking out for number one is an empty and futile goal. It is better to have said, "After all is said and done, more will have been done than said." That is commitment.

To believe in yourself may feel like confidence, but when taken to the extreme, it is most always interpreted by others as arrogance. Truly humble people believe in Someone bigger than themselves—God. They are committed to Him, and it shows.

I worked with a minister of music in Memphis, Tennessee. A man whose judgment I trusted said of him, "He's not flashy, but he wears well." He proved to be responsible, conscientious, and dedicated. At first, I hardly knew he was there. Through the months I found him more and more reliable. As I have reflected on that interim pastor experience, he modeled one of the main ingredients of a commitment to Christ.

Four ingredients Shadrach, Meshach, and Abednego had are worth modeling: *hope,* a vision to see what will become of us; *courage,* a determination to act out the vision in the face of great risk; *works,* actions speak louder than words; and *commitment,* a belief in Someone bigger than ourselves.

Notes

1. Don Devoe going as interim coach to Florida after having been fired at Tennessee in the same conference.

2. *The Interpreter's Bible*, vol. 6 (Nashville: Abingdon Press, 1953), 403.

12

The Minister and the Green-Eyed Monster

"'Saul has slain his thousands, and David his tens of thousands'" (1 Sam. 18:7).

"It gnaws! It gnaws!'

In Nathaniel Hawthorne's tale "The Bosom Serpent" he talks of the man of jealousy who holds his hand to his bosom and exclaims, "It gnaws! It gnaws!" He was known as the man with the snake in his breast. Indeed, that's what jealousy does: It gnaws.

His wife pleaded with him. He fell to the ground. There was a sound of rustling grass. The serpent crawled to the fountain, and he was cursed. The snake disappeared after a small tinkling sound in the fountain. Oh, that it could be that easy!

He drove me to the motel. He was under fire by his church. As we passed each church along the way, he told me of the pastor's shortcomings. This one was a radical. That one was a tyrant. Another was a Milquetoast.

"Who's doing a good job" I asked.

"Not many!" he said.

The Greek language has two words for anger: *orga* and *parorgismos*. *Orga* is the kind of anger that is natural and normal. *Para* is a prefix meaning "around." *Parorgismos* is the wrath that builds a wall around anger and keeps it.

Ephesians 4:26 reads "Be ye angry [*orga*], and sin not: let not the sun go down upon your wrath [*parorgismos*]" (KJV). That's what jealousy does. It builds a wall around normal feelings of *deficiency* and makes others the culprit. Jealousy is a derivative of anger: He or she has it, I don't.

I am not as good as you; therefore, something is wrong with you becomes the message. You sing better than I. I will find a flaw.

"'Saul has slain his thousands, and David his tens of thousands'" (1 Sam. 18:7). David said, "I have not wronged you, but you are hunting me down to take my life" (24:11). Jealousy has no reason. Jealousy is humiliating. It is indiscriminate and addictive. It isolates and is suicidal.

Some Characteristics to Know About Jealousy

Jealousy Is Indiscriminate

David was politically less than Saul. It did not matter. Saul was jealous.

Some pastors of small churches are natural targets of jealousy by pastors of larger churches if they are loved more. The size of the church is immaterial to the jealous person. However, some incur jealousy because of more visibility. Jealousy is indiscriminate.

Jealousy Is Addictive

You get hooked on it and keep nursing it. Saul said, "'You are more righteous than I'" (1 Sam. 24:17). He was repentant. A short time later he went back to his old ways. He took 3,000 men to the Desert of Ziph to kill David (26:2). He couldn't stop. He was obsessive and bent on destroying the object of his jealousy.

Edwin Stanton was jealous of Abraham Lincoln. He called him the "original gorilla" during the time when evolution was a political football. Still, Lincoln chose him as Secretary of War because he was the best man for the job. Stanton fought his addictive jealousy, but he continued saying unkind things about Lincoln even after he had been named Secretary of War.

As Stanton stood over the assassinated president's body he said, "There lies the greatest ruler of men who has lived since Jesus Christ." He was addicted to jealousy, but the better part of him finally knew the stature of Lincoln.

Jealousy Isolates

No one enjoys being around jealous people. They become social lepers. "'The Philistines are fighting against me, and God has turned away from me. He no longer answers me, either by prophets or by dreams" (1 Sam. 28:15).

Samuel said, "Why have you disturbed me . . . ?" (v. 1).

Saul's response: "'I am in great distress.'" Jealousy brings distress and isolation. Saul's own son Jonathan joined David's supporters because Saul's jealousy alienated him.

Jealousy Is Suicidal

Jealousy is self-destructive. It is a death wish. I can't compete with other's skills; therefore, I will resent others' skills. I can't celebrate my skills because I long for other's skills. That is suicidal. I can't enjoy being loved because I am not loved in the same way as others. That is suicidal. "So Saul took his own sword and fell on it" (1 Sam. 31:4).

He was bright, handsome, and talented. He had been a minister of music. He was now a banker. With each desperate attempt he failed in winning the affection of his best friend's wife. His own family was adoring and affectionate. It did not matter. His **jealousy** was **indiscriminate**. It did not matter that she was his best friend's wife. His jealousy was **addictive**. He pleaded with her for years. His jealousy **isolated** him. Slowly he lost his church and friends. Ultimately, his jealousy was **suicidal**. He took his own life

Ultimately, Only God Can Deal with Jealousy

• *Put on the new self.* You will have feelings of envy. Do not build a wall around it. "Put on the new self" (Eph. 4:24). God can deal with it. Jealousy is a disease. The antibiotic may be slow. God's love works miracles, but not easily. "Put on the new self."

• *Let God deal with the acclaim of others.* It will put jealousy to rest.

• *Join in the accolades of others.* At first, it will be awkward. Eventually the new self will help us affirm them.

• *Appreciate others' skills.* We are not all alike. We each have been given separate gifts and skills.

• *Avoid the "trap" of comparison.* God made each of us unique, not alike.

• *Avoid building self-esteem by diminishing others' attributes.*

• *Forgive.* The ultimate remedy for jealousy is seen in Ephesians 4:32: "Be kind and compassionate to one another, forgiving each other, just as in Christ God forgave you." Forgiveness is the only sure cure for jealousy. Try it!

Note

1. Nathaniel Hawthorne, "The Bosom Serpent," *McCartney's Illustrations,* ed. Clarence E. McCartney (New York: Abingdon, 1955), 194.

13

The Merits of Mediocrity

"I appeal to you for my son Onesimus who became my son while I was in chains. Formerly he was useless to you, but now he has become useful both to you and to me" (Philem. 10-11).

> "Either man's work or his own gifts; who best
> Bear his mild yoke, they serve him best. His state
> Is kingly; thousands at his bidding speed,
> And post o'er land and ocean without rest;
> They also serve who only stand and wait."[1]

In a world that emphasizes power and status, we often overlook the "unimportant" people. They're the ones who can't give large sums of money or help us move to a bigger church. We may be tempted to see them as average, mediocre people—just like Onesimus. But the story of Onesimus can teach us some things about the merits of mediocrity.

Let me quickly add that *mediocrity* does not refer here to the value of the person. I'm using it in comparison to those who have great wealth, influence, education, or social status.

Onesimus was not a celebrity evangelist. He pastored no large church in the Midwest. He had never been president of a national or state organization.

We have no indication he could speak eloquently, do great deeds, sing, or perform feats of strength. He was a mediocre man who had been caught in a sin.

Paul was a supporter of Onesimus. Onesimus could do very little for him politically. Philemon was the person of influence. Onesimus had been Philemon's slave. Evidently, Onesimus had robbed or stolen, perhaps from Philemon, and run away. He was converted to Christ while in the presence of Paul. He ministered to Paul.

Though we may call it other things, **a minister must be political**. He must share pertinent information with the legitimizers in a church. He must spend time with the people who make things happen. It is one of the unwritten responsibilities of the minister. We teach it only briefly in seminaries. We learn it quickly in ministering in a church. If you want to stay for a period of time in a church, you must be political.

Now it is not immoral to be political. Politicians may have given us a raw deal. When one thinks of being political, one thinks of getting something we do not deserve. But, that is not how it works. The people who make things happen are usually the people who care deeply for the church and its welfare. Occasionally, these people covet power, but it is not so frequent as we would have others believe.

However, Onesimus was just the opposite. He could not benefit Paul. Philemon was the person with whom Paul had to be political. Onesimus was a person of mediocrity in terms of political power, but he was not a person of mediocrity in terms of value to God.

Mediocre People Are Comfortable to Be With

"I am sending him—who is my very heart—back to you. I would have liked to keep him with me so that he could take your place in helping me while I am in chains" (vv. 12-13).

Mediocre People Learn to Make the Best of Bad Situations

"Formerly he was useless to you, but now he has become useful both to you and to me" (v. 11). There is a folk song that tells the story of a man whose wife is involved with the milkman. He permits the situation to continue for several years. A friend confronts him with the reality of the situation. "Well, I'm making the best of a bad situation. We get all the free milk, cheese, and yogurt we can use."

The second verse of the song tells about a woman married to a man who thought he was a "chicken." He pecked in the yard, scratching the dirt, and clucked a lot. When confronted about the necessity to do something about him, she replied, "I'm making the best of a bad situation. He doesn't eat much; he doesn't cluck after dark . . . and besides, we need the eggs." Making the best of a bad situation.

Onesimus made the best of a bad situation. He cleaned up his life. He began a life of service by attending Paul. His life of mediocrity had become a life of indispensability. If you want to serve, you must pay the piper—train, learn, and grow. Get prepared.

Mediocre People Are Growing People

Some people are "too learned" to grow. Some are too smart. Some are too gifted. Some are too wealthy. However, mediocre people are growing people. "Perhaps the reason he was separated from you for a little while was that you might have him back for good—no longer as a slave, but better than a slave, as a dear brother" (vv. 15-16).

Their status changes. They risk change in their lives. They are more fun to be with because they are searching for better ways to live their lives.

Mediocrity Is Not a Cop-Out

Onesimus was going back to face the music. He was not planning on spending his life with Paul, even though that would be more comfortable.

The Book of Philemon is a letter of commendation and recommendation. It was a plea to get Onesimus back in the good graces of Philemon. "So if you consider me a partner, welcome him as you would welcome me" (v. 17). He adds, "If he has done you any wrong or owes you anything, charge it to me" (v. 18).

Onesimus was not exceptional in any way except in the love that Paul had for him. He had become important to Paul.

"Be careful who you stick your neck out for," my Dad told me early on. I have had some close friends disgraced. That has not changed my concern and compassion for them. That has not changed my love for them. Most have risen above the disgrace. Those who have risen above the disgrace chose not to cop-out on life. They have started again in another vocation. Or they have started again in another kind of ministry. People with mediocre talent frequently become exceptional in their desire to be useful in life once they choose not to cop-out.

There Is Great Value in the Person Even Though His or Her work Is Mediocre

Paul stuck his neck out for Onesimus. Paul wrote with his own hand. He reminded Philemon that he owed him his "very self" (v. 19).

Paul was "confident of your obedience" (v. 21). He encouraged the loyalty of Philemon. And one thing more, "I'm coming to see you, so get a guest room ready for me."

Paul stood up for Onesimus. He tested the friendship of a longtime political friend. Philemon could wield influence for Paul. Onesimus could not. Paul's integrity is seen best in his willingness to commend Onesimus.

Conclusion

God looks at us and sees what others may never see. We may see ourselves as mediocre. God sees us as very special. Our work may not be exceptional or remarkable, but we are. We may not be politically powerful or financially persuasive, but God knows our heart and He writes a letter of commendation for us to the world. He sees us as we could be.

Two preachers had attended a state evangelism conference. One said, "I can preach better than any person I heard today, but no one will ever know."

His friend said, "You are wrong; your church already knows, and God knows. Incidentally, I know."

Even in our mediocrity, some persons have the gift of making you feel ten feet tall. Mrs. Rollins was one of those persons. She told me once, while still in grade school, "God has something very special planned for you." It meant little then, but it has guided my life many times when I have almost taken serious detours. Paul was that kind of friend to Onesimus. You can be that kind of friend to someone. Someone needs you. They may not be able to do much for you, but God expects that kind of friendship out of each of us. Unselfish devotion to a friend may be the warmest gift you will ever give.

Note

1. John Milton, "On His Blindness," in *Eerdman's Book of Christian Poetry,* comp. Pat Alexander (Grand Rapids: Wm. B. Eerdmans Publishing Co., 1981), 31.

14

The Final Four

"Put on the full armor of God so that you can take your stand against the devil's schemes" (Eph. 6:11).

"Look at your past victories. You've no reason to feel depressed."[1]

Four teams competed for the NCAA Championship of 1990: Georgia Tech; Duke; University of Nevada, Las Vegas; and Arkansas. When you reach the Final Four, it's time to "put up or shut up." It's time to "lay it on the line." It's time to "take your best shot." All the clichés in basketball are appropriate. "No pain, no gain." "No guts, no glory."

The week before, Vanderbilt University won its first National Invitational Tournament (NIT). No sooner had Coach Eddie Fogler stepped off the plane in Nashville than a reporter asked, "What are you going to do for an encore?"

It never ends. You win, but it is temporary. Personally, I am a great winner. I am a terrible loser. I walked the yard during the game between Vanderbilt University and St. Louis University. My son watched for me. I taped it. I have since watched it four times. I couldn't stand the thought of losing. When Vanderbilt was ahead seventeen points, I just knew we were going to lose. I am a terrible loser.

Sixty-three teams in the NCAA will end their season with a loss. Only one will keep winning. Actually, two will win with the NIT. What is on the docket for an encore? What is there to look forward to for the losers? What can the winner do for an encore? It's the American way.

Ninety-year-old Maude was at the doctor complaining about aches and pains. "You're in good condition for your age; now about those aches and pains. I can't make you any **younger**," the doctor told her.

Maude replied, "I don't want to get any **younger**; I want to get **older**." It's hard to celebrate the past when the future is so uncertain.

Anyone, including me, can support a winner. Anyone can support a success. Only a great person will continue to have faith in a failure. When Vanderbilt lost seven straight games, my wife kept saying they would come back. I didn't believe her. I had already given up. I had decided this was the last time we buy season tickets. She supported the failures. I am a success supporter. You never know who will emerge a winner. You never know how important the wins have been if you only concentrate on the last loss.

Will Campbell tells a story of an Easter chicken in *Brother to a Dragon Fly*. A cute purple chicken was given to a little girl. As it grew it began to look weird after Easter. The color faded. The chicken had a hard time in the pen with the other chickens. They would peck on its head and edge the Easter chicken away from the feeding tray. They soon discovered their purple chicken was larger than they. It had an air of self-confidence. It became thoroughly at home even though it did not look like the others. It had been a loser. Now it handled itself like a winner. In reality, it grew into a Rhode Island Red, a chicken much more valuable than any in the chicken yard. Real winners can take the temporary losses. Ultimately, they know they will win.

The teams in the Final Four are there because they believed in themselves. There are no losers in the Final Four. They have survived. They have fought the battles. They know the odds.

Deanna Harrison told the wonderful story of Elijah in her book *My Ducks Are Really Swans*. In her words, God said to Elijah, "Look at your past victories. You've no reason to feel depressed."[2]

Paul wrote to the Ephesians, "Put on the full armor of God so that you can take your stand against the devil's schemes" (6:11).

Four Ingredients

There are at least four ingredients to get to the Final Four. These are also applicable to life: conditioning, uniforms, defense, and offense.

Conditioning

Conditioning is preparation, personal growth, and learning. "Be strong in the Lord" (v. 10). Why? Because there is "struggle." The "struggle" is against the spiritual forces of evil in the heavenly realms.

"Serve wholeheartedly" (v. 7) means to have *respect* for the coach's directions. John Feinstein wrote a scathing exposé of Indiana basketball and Bobby

Knight, their coach, in *Season on the Brink*. Though you may not agree with Knight's philosophy, you have to respect his demand for conditioning. Teams cannot win without conditioning. "You gotta be ready," he has said on more than one occasion.

Without conditioning, adversity will crumble even the strongest. "Serve wholeheartedly" means prepare your body to the best of your ability.

The Christian who does not condition his or her spiritual life to living cannot face adversity. These persons end up whining and complaining when the crises strike, and the crises will strike. Sooner or later everyone has an opportunity to go to the foul line with four seconds left and the game on the line. Conditioning will determine readiness.

For the Christian this means giving your best. Pray without ceasing. Love when it is easier to be vindictive. Forgive when it is easier to hold a grudge. Listen when it is easier to defend. Pray. Live respectfully. Serve wholeheartedly.

"Be strong in the Lord" (v. 10). You cannot be strong in the Lord without the conditioning of the Christian life. You have to practice the Ten Commandments, not just study them. You have to live by the Sermon on the Mount, not simply teach it.

Uniforms

Uniforms identify teams. Uniforms also equip players for their task. Football players wear helmets, pads, and cleated shoes. Without this equipment, they could not play well or safely. "Put on the full armor of God," Paul says (v. 11). You must be able to identify the players by their uniform.

We must model Christ. It is not enough to condition ourselves. We must put on the uniform. We must show others that we are Christians.

It is important how others see us. If we live extravagantly, we show others we have disdain for poverty. If we exploit others, we do not model Christ. Serving others means we put on the full armor of God by loving, caring, forgiving, and winning. We are the model of Christ. We place the uniforms of His compassion on our lives, or we make mockery of what He stood for.

The uniform of Christ is integrity; a person not divided against himself or herself. The uniform of Christ is honesty. We do not lie to others' or ourselves. The uniform of Christ is unselfishness. We care for others needs, not just our own. The uniform of Christ is love. We love when we are unloved. We love because He first loved us.

Defense

Defense means being unintimidated; having integrity, morality, ethics, and loyalty, being able to work through anger. "You may be able to stand your ground" (v. 13).

Reaching back for a strength you did not know you had is defense. There is no glory in reaching for that strength. There is no glory in defense. There is only unselfish fulfilling of obligation, responsibility, and service.

The best defensive team rarely gets credit. Perhaps the best defensive team in the Southeastern Conference was Alabama. They played tough, unselfish, and hard-nosed defense. Like Tennessee in football, the defense did not get the credit of the press, but they paid the price. The end result showed it.

In the Christian life, the defense is rarely recognized. These are the loyal people. Give me a person who serves devotedly for a model of Christianity. These are not simply the glorified converted prostitutes, drug addicts, and thieves. These are the people in the trenches. These are the people who have served even when there is no glory. My hero is someone who has paid the price of faithfulness.

Perhaps it is true that the best defense is a good offense, but I doubt it. It is only the good defensive teams that reach their full potential.

Offense

Offense means hard work, being a self-starter and conscientious "with your feet fitted with the readiness that comes from the gospel of peace" (v. 15). Also, "pray in the Spirit on all occasions" (v. 18).

Map out a plan. Maximize your efforts. Know your direction.

The Memphis State basketball team has a trick play. If they have possession on the inbounds play to begin the second half, they line up under the opponent's basket. This decoys the other team into thinking they will have an offensive play on the wrong basket. Then the one lone guard takes the ball the opposite direction to lay it in. It worked several times during the past year. They knew the direction, even if the opponent did not.

Paul knew the importance of a good offense. "Pray also for me, that whenever I open my mouth, words may be given me so that I will fearlessly make known the mystery of the gospel" (v. 19). It is important to take the word of Christ to the world.

You cannot sit in church and expect your church to grow. You cannot wait for the lost to come without beckoning. You must take the offensive. You must take the gospel of Christ to the world.

Lots of folks want friends, but an offense means you must make the effort to be a friend. Lots of folks want to be in condition, but you have to exercise. Take the offensive. Lots of folks want to lose weight, but you have to take the offensive to cut back on food. Lots of folks want more money, but you have to take the offensive in managing the money you have to get it. Lots of folks want to be good Christians, but you have to take the offensive in being like Christ. You cannot submit to your own selfish desires and wants and be like Christ. It is hard work.

Sixty-three teams will lose. One will win. To see all sixty-four as winners takes a real vision. You can be a winner without winning the National Championship. How? Conditioning, uniforms, defense, and offense.

Notes

1. Deanna Harrison, *My Ducks Are Really Swans* (Nashville: Broadman, 1988), 63.
2. Ibid.

15

Uncertainty Is the Only Thing Certain

"I will not leave you" (John 14:18).

"Death and taxes are certain, but so is God's love."

A man was being interviewed for work with the FBI. He was "uncertain" about a lot of things.

Q: "How much is one and one?"
A: "Eleven."
Q: "Well, that's not exactly what we had in mind, but your mind may be more analytical than we thought."
Q: "How many days in the week start with *T?*"
A: "Two."
Q: "Correct. What are they?"
A: "Today and tomorrow."
Q: "Well, you've got a sense of humor. That's not bad. You'll need it."
A: "Thank you."
Q: "Who killed Abraham Lincoln?"
A: "I don't know."
Q: "That's OK. Can you find out?"
A: "Sure."

When he went home his wife asked how it went. "Great. They asked easy questions and I've been assigned to a murder case," he replied.

That is uncertainty. But we have uncertainty, too. Can we pay our taxes? Can we pay our bills? Can we pay for our children's college education? Are we secure in our work? Will Social Security be enough to live on? Will I make money from some investments? Will my kids still love me when I'm too old to help them? Will my spouse ever learn to do dishes? Will my children ever clean their rooms? Will I ever get the kitchen floor clean again? Will I ever get my husband to put the dirty dishes in the dishwasher?

The disciples were concerned and uncertain about weightier things.

• *Being alone (John 13:36).* Being abandoned is terrifying. My granddaughter, Brooke, walked away from me after several requests for her not to. I stepped around the corner to hide.

"Pawpaw," she said with uneasiness in her voice. Being alone is terrifying. It was a dumb trick. I learned quickly.

• *Uncertainty about the future (John 14:1-2).* Someone else will die, not me. However, we know **down deep** we will die. The ultimate question is: "Where will I go after death?"

• *Uncertainty about the process (John 14:15).* Jesus called Himself "the life" to Martha, "the door" to the Pharisees, and "the light" in John 8:12. Here He is *hodos*—"the way," the process. Trust Christ and you don't have to be uncertain about anything. He is the way, the road map.

How to Be Certain About Uncertainty

Have Confidence in Your Ability to Survive

"It won't kill you" may be words to live by. Worry is wasted energy. Death and taxes are certainties. Worry is an option.

Get Outside Yourself

Believe in something bigger than your own ability. Most self-helps are rip-offs. Don't look within for strength. You'll worry yourself to death trying to come up with survival techniques. Look outside. God is bigger than your best day. He is certainly bigger than your worse day. Trust Him to help you.

Look Around, Not Past

Some people are so preoccupied with the uncertainty of life that they miss the life in front of them. "Show us the Father." "Don't you know me?" "My husband doesn't love me." "You mean thirty-seven years with you doesn't say anything?" "You say I don't love you. How many ways do I have to say it?"

It is chic to say, "Nobody loves me," but spare me. Save it for Oprah, Donahue, and Geraldo.

Look at the Evidence (John 14:11)

Look at the evidence that surrounds you: the building, gathering, sounds of music, words of worship, the proclamation of Christ, the miracle of healing, and the miracle of regeneration. Look at the evidence. You can be certain about evidence: creation, sunshine, rain, flowers, morning, evening, joy, laughter, reunion, and hope. You can trust the evidence. In that you can be certain.

You May Be Alone. You Do Not Have to Be Lonely

"I will not leave you as orphans; I will come to you" (John 14:18). You can be certain, Brooke, I will not leave you. Your Pawpaw cares. He will not leave you.

The commitment of marriage is that you will not leave the other person. The commitment of parenting is that you will not forsake your children when they need you. The commitment of senior years is that you will not forsake your family and friends. You may be alone, but you do not have to be lonely.

Live Expectantly

Jesus is truth *(alētheia),* life *(zōē),* and peace *(ereinē).* The opposite is to live with dread and fear. There is no fear in love.

Living expectantly is waiting eagerly for the good things to happen. Things are rough now, but ultimately God and I will win. You may lose one game, but there will be another. You may have a losing season, but there will be another. Those are not empty words. If your spouse loses his or her faculties, live courageously, but live expectantly. God will give you strength. He may not take away the pain, but He will give you strength to live with the pain. Live expectantly.

16

Moses Was Not an NBA Superstar

"God called to him from within the bush" (Ex. 3:4).

"A true and safe leader is likely to be one who has no desire to lead, but is forced into a position of leadership by the inward pressure of the Holy Spirit and the press of the external situation. Such were Moses and David."

—A. W. Tozer

Moses Malone is an NBA superstar with the Atlanta Hawks. He delivered the 76ers out of oblivion. Moses in the Bible did not have the same gifts that Moses Malone had, but he delivered the Hebrew children out of bondage.

In an interview Michael Jordan said,

Six years into my professional career, I have accepted the role of leader. When I first broke into the league, the role was uncomfortable. I was expected to do more than I thought I could. I could play, but knew little about leading.

What Makes a Great Leader?

Enthusiasm, optimism, persistence, ambition, competitiveness, knowledge, insight, inquisitiveness, independence, friendliness, adventurousness, security, decisiveness, integrity, flexibility, sense of humor, discipline, creativity, practicality, aggressiveness, and poise make a great leader.

Leadership qualities can be found in Acts 6 and 1 Timothy 3:1-13.

Above reproach, the husband of but one wife, temperate, self-controlled, respectable, hospitable, able to teach, not given to drunkenness, not violent but gentle, not quarrelsome, not a lover of money. He must manage his own family well and see that his children obey him with proper respect. . . . He must not be a recent convert, or he may become conceited and fall under the same judgment as the devil. He must also have a good reputation with outsiders, so that he will not fall into disgrace and into the devil's trap (1 Tim. 3:2-4,6-7).

Jeremiah 45:5 says: "Should you then seek great things for yourself? Seek them not." Those who seek to be great leaders seldom become one.

"For not from the east, nor from the west, Nor from the desert comes exaltation; But God is the Judge; He puts down one, and exalts another" (Ps. 75:6-7, NASB).

Some are born to become leaders. Others have leadership thrust upon them, such as Moses. Here are some characteristics of Moses, who had superstardom thrust upon him.

Instinct for Justice (Ex. 2:11-17)

He protected his own. He rescued seven girls who wanted to fill their water troughs for their flocks.

Moses was not a **blister.** Some people are like blisters; they never show up until after the work is done. Moses was their leader, even before he recognized it. He did not wait for the afterglow. He was there when the work was to be done.

Shakespeare once said, "He is well paid that is well satisfied." Moses was not looking for praise. He was already getting into hot water. He was, however, satisfied with his instinct for justice.

If you don't like what you're doing, you'll never get paid enough. If you love what you're doing, you'd do it for free.

Moses Was Called (Ex. 3:1-6)

He was unmistakably selected by God. These are the best "credentials." Training comes next. Ministers must have the credentials by the calling before they are trained for the working. Leaders who do not have God's call are asking for a malcontented history in ministry.

Moses Was a Reluctant Leader (Ex. 3:11—4:1)

This is called **humility.** It must be genuine. It must be a life-style. He told God, "I'm not the man for the job." He also complained, "What if they do not believe me or listen to me and say 'The Lord did not appear to you'?" (4:1).

If God is on your side, it is always lopsided against your enemies. "But Moses pleaded, 'O Lord, O Lord, I'm just not a good speaker. I never have been, and I'm not now, even after you have spoken to me, for I have a speech impediment.'" But God responded, "Who makes mouths?" (4:10, author).

However, God sent Aaron to help him anyway. God always provides an option, even though He never needs one. God's options are gifts to the neurotic needs of His leaders.

Charles Swindoll writes that all great ideas go through three channels:

- *Rejection.* "It won't work." "We've tried it before."
- *Toleration.* "Well, I'll allow it, as long as . . ."
- *Acceptance.* "Let's go!"

Moses Was in the Right Place at the Right Time

That makes a great leader. You have to be there when it happens. Ball players call it "rising to the occasion during crunch time."

One night a ship's captain saw what looked like the lights of another ship heading toward him. He asked his signalman to blink, "Change your course ten degrees south."

The reply was, "Change **your** course ten degrees north."

The captain sent a second message: "I am a captain. Change your course south."

"Well, I am a seaman first class. Change your course north," the sailor replied.

Infuriated, the captain said with an oath, "I say change your course south. I'm on a battleship."

The reply was, "And I say change your course north. I'm in a lighthouse."

A good leader is in the right place at the right time.

Proverbs 16:9 says, "The mind of man plans his way, But the Lord direct his steps" (NASB).

Moses Was the Messenger of God

He turned a rod into a serpent, so did the sorcerers. He turned the Nile to blood, so did the sorcerers. He brought hordes of frogs, so did the sorcerers. Then the sorcerers ran out of ammunition. The messenger of God can always reload. Moses brought lice, flies, plagues, boils, locusts, darkness, and death to the sons. "But use the blood of the lamb on the two side frames on the door . . . and I will pass over" (Ex. 12:6-8, author).

The Lord's Supper has its beginning here. "This annual celebration with unleavened bread will cause you always to remember today as the day when I brought you out of the land of Egypt" (12:17, author).

Moses Learned to Cope with Bickering (Ex. 15:24)

"Then the people turned against Moses. Must we die of thirst? Weren't there enough graves in Egypt that you brought us out here to die"(15:24, author).

Then in 16:2-3, they got bitter, "Oh, that we were back in Egypt, and that the

Lord had killed us there. For there we had plenty to eat. But now you have brought us into this wilderness to kill us with starvation" (author).

Moses cried the cry of every minister: "What shall I do? For they are almost ready to stone me." He "struck" the rock in his impatience. The water came, but they named the place Meribah, meaning "argument" or "strife" because that is what Meribah means in Hebrew.

Everybody wants to tell a football coach what is wrong if the team loses. Alex Agase, a college football coach said, "If you really want to give me advice, do it on Saturday afternoon between one and four o'clock, when you've got twenty-five seconds to do it, between plays. Don't give me advice on Monday. I know the right thing to do on Monday." Bickering is usually done by those who are afraid to get involved in the sticky decision-making process.

Roger Rose, of the Rancho Santa Fe School in California, spoke to a commencement audience. "You can probably divide people into two kinds: 'You won't; you can't,' and 'I will; I can.'"

The first kind are bickerers. The second type cope. The minister who has not learned to cope with bickering will be eternally miserable.

Moses Distributed the Work Load

He gave away his glory. He shared the accolades. He got no kicks from having people depend upon him. Exodus 18:21 records that Jethro counseled Moses not to try to judge every dispute that arose. Instead, Moses should select leaders and place them over thousands, hundreds, fifties, and tens.

Winston Churchill divided the work force. He told Roosevelt in a speech February 9, 1941, during a radio broadcast: "Give us the tools, and we will finish the job."[1] On another occasion Churchill said,

> I have nothing to offer but blood, toil, tears, and sweat. We shall not flag or fail. We shall go on to the end. We shall fight in France, we shall fight in the seas and oceans, we shall fight with growing confidence and growing strength in the air; we shall defend our Island whatever the cost may be. We shall fight on the beaches, we shall fight on the landing grounds, we shall fight in the fields and in the streets, we shall fight in the hills; we shall never surrender.[2]

The all-inclusive word he used was *we*. He shared the load, and they followed.

Someone described leadership this way: "If you want to see a leader—a real leader—check to see if there are those who follow."

A real leader must:

- have an instinct for justice,
- be called,
- face leadership with reluctance (humility),
- be in the right place at the right time,
- be the messenger of God
- learn to cope with bickering, and
- distribute the work load.

There are leaders here today. Will you take charge, and lead your church in reaching people for Christ, growing people in Christ, and managing the work load as it is done? You don't have to be an NBA superstar to do that. Einstein's brain was the same size as yours. An autopsy proved it. God can do wonders with an ordinary person like Moses or you!

Notes

1. In John Bartlett, *Familiar Quotations* (Boston: Little, Brown, and Co., 1955), 570.
2. Dorothy Price and Dean Walley, *Never Give In!* (Kansas City: Hallmark Cards, Inc., 1976), 3-4, 6.

17

Everyone Needs a Best Friend?

"A friend is one who takes the side with the sun in his eyes."
—Charlie Brown

"A friend loves at all times" (Prov. 17:17).

"A man of many companions may come to ruin, but there is a friend who sticks closer than a brother" (Prov. 18:24).

Can you name your best friend? Some can; some can't! Jonathan could. "Jonathan said to David, 'Whatever you want me to do, I'll do it for you'" (1 Sam. 20:4). Recently, I spoke on the importance of friendship to others. The best biblical example that I know is Jonathan. Jesus said it best, "Greater love has no one than this, that he lay down his life for his friends" (John 15:13).

Define a *Friend*

A *friend* watches the television program you want to watch. A friend puts himself down but not you. A friend listens without feeling the compulsion to tell you about her troubles. A friend withholds judgment. A friend supports you when you're in the wrong, but doesn't condone the wrong you have done.

This devotional is about another kind of friend: yourself. Mildred Newman and Bernard Berkowitz wrote a bestseller entitled *How to Be Your Own Best Friend*. It's about making a friend of yourself.

Jesus said, "'Blessed are the poor in spirit'" (Matt. 5:3). Blessed are the spiritually impoverished. This takes on a new light when we see it as meaning, "Blessed are those who know their deficiencies but are not destroyed by them." These people own the kingdom of heaven. Blessedness *(makarios)* is happiness, of course. If you are to be happy, you must stop putting yourself down. You must begin doing the things that make you have respect for yourself. Without God, we are impoverished. With God, we are spiritual giants. Blessed is the person who does not feel the need to tell others they are spiritual giants.

Newman and Berkowitz wrote, "When Thoreau remarked that most men live lives of quiet desperation, he could not have foreseen how noisy that desperation would become."[1] It is not in quiet desperation but in noisy hysteria that we often live our lives. We would rather tell others about our unhappiness than how we have learned to cope. We need to look at how to be your own worst enemy.

Fear the Anticipated

"What next?" is more a theme than "I'm ready for what comes."

A man wanted to pet a dog. "Will your dog bite?" he asked.

"Absolutely not," the man replied.

The man began to pet the dog. The dog almost took a finger off. Pulling away in horror, the man screamed, "I thought you said your dog didn't bite!"

"It doesn't," was the reply. "That isn't my dog."

The unanticipated can be difficult. You can be your own worst enemy by being afraid of something.

Be Rigid

"Don't bend. Don't apologize. Both are a sign of weakness." Rigid people set themselves up for disappointment with ideas like these.

Erwin Tieman wrote, "Nothing influences the quality of our life more than how we respond to trouble."[2]

Rigid people know a lot about women's rights, men's rights, criminal rights, patient rights, labor rights, civil rights, animal rights, human rights, religious rights, and consumer rights; but they know little about the rights of others, of turning the other cheek, or God's rights. Rigid people respond to trouble by blaming others. It is our right to be rigid, but it is also one of the best ways to be our own worst enemy.

Have a "Microwave Mind-Set" in a "Conventional-Oven World"

"I want happiness, and I want it now." A young couple looks at their parents. "Why can't we have a house like yours *now?* The price of working to pay for it is too high to wait. "I want my husband cured of alcoholism now!" Why should I wait? "I want love and respect from my children now." Why should I wait?

You can live with twenty-eight-hour intentions in a twenty-four-hour day. It is your prerogative to be unhappy. You have a right to be your own worst enemy.

Try to Control the Important People in Your Life

"Here is what I want from my wife." That statement is a set up for misery. It is a self-styled trap.

My wife and I were driving over a beautiful highway on the landscape of Maui. The volcanic mountains covered with mist were on the left. The emerald green waters of the Pacific were on the right. The traffic was light. The weather was perfect. The sun was shining. "Look at those wonderful sailboats off the horizon," I told my wife.

Buried in the tour guide books, she replied, "It is thirteen minutes to the shopping center at Lahaina." You can't control the important people in your life. You set yourself up for disappointment. I love her anyway.

Be Your Own Best Friend

There Are No Quick Fixes

There are mountains to climb. There are loads to lift. There are tasks to be performed. However, there are no quick fixes. Don't believe in the fly-by-nights. Most people who look for magic switches are people looking in the wrong places. They buy too much for themselves to prove their worth. They do things over and over to make themselves feel good about themselves but to no avail.

People who hate themselves "the morning after" should ask a simple question: "What quick fix did I seek the night before?" If wallowing in self-reproach the following day is our idea of being our best friend, we should have serious doubts about what we are doing for ourselves.

It is true some feel good about feeling bad. They try a quick fix of continuing a bad relationship or destroying another by gossip. They may be saying, "I'm a terrible person, and I like it that way. Leave me alone." Strangely enough, there are some like that. Remember, when you try a quick fix you get a false sense of feeling good about yourself. You become an enemy not a friend.

Meet Your Own Expectations

Don't set your expectations so high that they are unreal. Recognize your own capabilities. Know your possibilities. If you do not have the resources to build a new home with then take pleasure in building the home you can afford. Take pleasure in doing the job you can do and have the resources to do.

Why did James and John want to debate the issue of "place" at Jesus' feet?

Perhaps one reason is that they had the same thing we do—unrealistic expectations. Not everyone can be Billy Graham, nor should they want to. God has a place for us. We should know our expectations.

If You Don't Have Love You Can't Give It

Learn how important you are to God. Learn the importance of self-respect and self-regard. Self-esteem is not in measuring ourselves with others. Self-esteem is in finding how we fit into the scheme of God's plan. Love yourself because God loves us. Then you can love others. Without self-regard, you cannot give love to others.

Self-denial is not a feeling of worthlessness. Giving up things for others while feeling resentful because we gave it up is the worst form of manipulation. We want others to know how much we sacrificed for them. That is not self-denial; that is exploitation. "Look what I've done for you. I'm so unselfish." Self-denial is giving to others without regard for appreciation.

Rid Yourself of Self-Fulfilling Prophecies

"I am a terrible person. I do terrible things." People fulfill these prophecies. Turn it around. "I am a good person because God has saved me." "I am a decent person because I have adopted the model of Christ." Say these things and you will become them.

Children classified as low achievers tend to become low achievers. Aptitude tests are often a deterrent to learning abilities if interpreted incorrectly. Low achievers expect little of themselves. Get rid of labels. Labels are self-fulfilling prophecies.

Remember determination is different from willpower. *Determination* to **be** is a positive prophecy, while *willpower* is an effort to "keep from" and "not do." Willpower treats yourself with no respect. Determination is a high regard for yourself. Your natural self does not want to do things that are foreign to it; it wants to realize its own potential.

Ultimately, Remember You Are Loved

God loves us. It is simple and profound. It is difficult to believe. You can choose and believe you are unlovable. You can believe you are loved. You can believe you are nothing. You can believe you are something in God's plan.

One of William Faulkner's characters said, "Between grief and nothing, I'll take grief." The implication is that there are no other choices. However, there are other choices. You can choose hope, anticipation, growth, and development.

Also, you can choose grief or nothing—bad alternatives. I choose hope and the fact that God loves me.

Additionally, others love me, not everyone. The ones I want to love me don't always do, but enough people do to matter and make a difference. That's worth living for. That's worth being your own best friend.

In conclusion, be your own best friend. Don't look for quick fixes. Meet your own expectations. If you don't have love, you can't give it. Rid yourself of self-fulfilling prophecies, and remember you are loved. It will work.

Notes

1. Mildred Newman and Bernard Berkowitz, *How to Be Your Best Friend* (New York: Ballantine Books, 1970), 13.

2. Jose A. Freeman, *God Is Not Fair* (New York: Here's Life Publishers, 1987), 56.

18

A Little Robe from Mother

"Honor your father and your mother" (Ex. 20:12).

Mothers, here is a legitimate reason for gaining weight. It is seen in both of these passages (Ex. 20:12; Deut. 5:16). The word is *kabed*. Its translation is "to make heavy, weighty." There you have it.

"Make your father and mother heavy." Well, it also means to take your father and mother seriously, take the responsibility of your parents to heart, and give heavy consideration to your parents. It could mean to make your father and mother heavy. At least some parents seem to take that translation seriously.

Wilfred Funk, the author of several dictionaries once was asked to list the ten most impressive words in the English language.

1. The most bitter word is **alone**.
2. The most tragic word is **death**.
3. The most beautiful word is **love**.
4. The most cruel word is **revenge**.
5. The most peaceful word is **tranquil**.
6. The saddest word is **forgotten**.
7. The warmest word is **friendship**.
8. The coldest word is **no**.
9. The most comforting word is **faith**.
10. The most reverent word is **mother**.[1]

The most comforting Scripture to a mother is Genesis 2:24: "For this reason a man will leave his father and mother and be united to his wife." There is a time for everything, and a mother knows better than anyone when it is time for a child to get out of the house and leave his father and mother. Therefore the most comforting word to a mother may not be *faith* but *leave*.

"So the woman remained and nursed her son until she weaned him" (1 Sam.

1:23, NASB). "Each year his mother made him a little robe and took it to him" (2:19).

The word for mother in Hebrew is *Em*. *Emily* is mother. The word in Greek for mother is *meter,* pronounced *matar*—the "one who measures."

Robert Fulghum is a minister as well as a wonderful author. The pulpit is a place to try new things, but on Mother's Day he knew he'd better be traditional. He said,

> The expectations were summarized in these words of one of the more outspoken women in the church, "I'm bringing my mother to church on Mother's Day, Reverend, and you can talk about anything you want. But it had better include mother, and it had better be good."[2]

I've never been a mother. I have no right to speak or write on Mother's Day. Like many of you, I better include mother on Mother's Day, and I better be good. One hundred and forty million greeting cards are sold—very few humorous ones for Mother's Day. About seven billion dollars are spent for presents and taking mom out to eat. Sixty million roses are given, not to count orchids and potted plants. It is the biggest commercial activity for a holiday after Christmas and Easter. Only at Christmastime does the telephone company do more business.

Once we were playing a game about tapes our mothers left us. We heard many inspiring phrases from the participants: "You're my favorite." "You're not the best, but you're better than anyone else I know." "You're the smartest daughter on earth." "You're the prettiest daughter on earth." "You're the most handsome son in town." Then we got serious. "You must do the best you can." "Always try harder." "Dig a little deeper." "You can do better than that."

Erma Bombeck is my favorite mother. She says the saying she remembers best is, "I was only trying to help." That excuses a lot, doesn't it? Erma puts things in perspective. She doesn't make spiritual slogans out of family settings. She knows the difference in a pig in a poke and a child on the pedestal. She knows her children are both. It depends on how many cups of coffee she has had. She said on a talk show she wanted to be remembered as a mother who "survived." Her efforts to "do this for your sake" would be incredible.

Robert Fulghum offered some motherly thoughts:

    1. Children are not pets.

    2. The life they actually live and the life you perceive them to be living is not the same life.

    3. Don't take what your children do too personally.

    4. Don't keep scorecards on them—a short memory is useful.

5. Dirt and mess are a breeding ground for well-being.

6. Stay out of their rooms after puberty.

7. Stay out of their friendships and love-life unless invited in.

8. Don't worry that they never listen to you; worry that they are always watching you.

9. Learn from them; they have much to teach you.

10. Love them long; let them go early.[3]

Maybe the best advice a mother can give a child is from Fulghum, "Them that's going on with us, get out and push. Them that ain't, get out of the way."[4] How about this one for a tape: "Sit still—just sit still." Or "Sit down and shut up!" "Get out of my sight." We have said it, but we regret it.

Some mothers should learn to sit still for the sake of their children and human-kind. My granddaughter and I have a game. She is hyper when she is ready to go to bed. Our game is to start to be "quiet." We stop talking. We stop playing. We set the stage for rest and quiet. Jesus sat still in a garden. Gandhi and King sat still for the perfection of a powerful tool of social change. Mothers can sit still for the welfare of their children.

Be still and let them learn from their mistakes. Be still and let them grow in experimenting with life. Be still and let them learn the importance of being still. "Be still, and know that I am God" (Ps. 46:10).

Hannah dedicated Samuel. She had good advice for Samuel in her prayer (1 Sam. 2).

1. She rejoiced in the Lord (v. 1).

2. Don't be arrogant. Measure yourself by the works of God (vv. 2-3).

3. You will stumble; you will have strength enough to get up (v. 4).

4. Don't be afraid to work for others. "Those who are full hire themselves out for food" (v. 5). This is also planning ahead.

5. Don't lose your perspective in life. Some who are barren count the world as children. Some who have many sons still whine (v. 5b).

6. Life will balance out. "The Lord brings death and makes alive; he brings down to the grave and raises up. The Lord sends poverty and wealth; he humbles and he exalts" (vv. 6-7).

7. There is always hope. "He raises the poor from the dust and lifts the needy from the ash heap; he seats them with princes and has them inherit a throne of honor" (v. 8).

8. Power is relative and temporary. "It is not by strength that one prevails" (v. 9).

9. "Those who oppose the Lord will be shattered" (v. 10).

The beautiful aspect of motherhood is recorded in verse 19, "Each year his mother made him a little robe and took it to him when she went up with her husband to offer the annual sacrifice." *Sacrificial and thoughtful giving is the definition of motherhood.*

Mothers Become Heavy in Memory

Mothers become heavy in memory when they give the gift of affection like "a little robe" or changing their minds about their children who have become adults. A woman gave an explanation when she was arrested while driving her new car. She said, "I was making an "O" turn; I started to make a "U" turn and changed my mind."

When a mother changes her mind about the capacity of her child to accomplish, she makes an "O" turn about her children, and her children rejoice. Mothers give the gift of warning, even though often unappreciated, to their children.

A man wrote of a night flight to Chicago. He was accompanied by his boss. Fire was shooting out of the engine. Being an experienced traveler, the boss assured him the fire was normal. He had considered the possibility that he would be thought a fool before he considered waking his boss. His caring spirit was the stronger part of wisdom so he acted on it. The letter concluded, "Fire is coming out of the manifold." He wrote, "You have truly been a blessing to us and 'God done good' when he sent you." It was one of the nicest letters I ever received. Mothers need to give the gift of warning because it says **I care for you**. Warnings are often bittersweet, but they always say I care.

In conclusion, let me offer a few suggestions to you about your mother.

1. Love her in spite of her warts. She deserves it.
2. Let her know you enjoy her company by spending time with her.
3. Write her a letter, even if you live with her.
4. Let her be heavy in respect, adoration, and love.
5. Help her when she needs it, but don't force her to take it.
6. Encourage her in what she wants to do, not in what you want her to do.
7. Don't neglect her. Remember her.
8. Allow her to give a "little robe" to you now and then.
9. Don't downgrade her because she is older; "upgrade" her because she is older.
10. Remember to say, "I love you, I appreciate you. You're important to me." She gave you the most important gift: life.

My mom supported me even when I didn't deserve it.

She loved me even tho' I didn't earn it.

She never neglected me even if she felt like it.

I watched her wrath toward others; I never experienced it.

She still gives me "a little robe" every Mother's Day, tho' she's been dead for years.

She was Hannah even tho' her name was Ollie Lou.

Notes

1. Wilfred Funk, *Sunday Sermons*, May/June 1990, 19.

2. Robert Fulghum, *It was on Fire When I Lay Down On It* (New York: Villard Books, 1989), 100.

3. Ibid., 103.

4. Ibid., 109.

19

Sour Grapes or Individual Responsibility

"The fathers have eaten sour grapes, and the children's teeth are set on edge" (Jer. 31:29).

"Blaming parents is the easiest cop-out on responsibility."

I'm tired of "pretentious" drama about child abuse, aren't you? The abuse of a child is not drama when the theme is exploited. It has been milked by Oprah, Donahue, King, and Geraldo. The titillating theme sucks a mentally or morally deficient America into the jaws of greed. It becomes talk-show themes. We are often best at feeling "ain't it awful!"

It would seem the cause of our problems is the sins of our parents. Some therapists have encouraged this myth.

A son is in the drunk tank, and the parents are called by the police. The first utterance by the mother: "What did we do wrong?" Sound familiar?

In the light of this "sour grapes" philosophy, see the *Teenage Mutant Ninja Turtle* phenomenon now so prevalent. It is the magnetic charm of contradiction. We are amused and attracted to contradiction. Turtles move slowly; ninjas move fast. How is a Ninja Turtle possible? It's not. That's what is so intriguing.

An intellectual, an outdated hippie, a turtle with a Spanish accent, and one with an Eastern accent is an unlikely, incredible, intriguing, and irresistible combination to millions of children between the ages of seven and twelve.

It's the **contradiction**.

Therapists call it "paradoxical intention"—doing it exactly backwards—the contradiction. Tony was three; Missy was four. Tony would eat virtually nothing but cereal. We worried about his nutritional balance. What could we do, we wondered.

John Hendrix had just finished his Ph.D. and had been studying Victor Frankl's "Paradoxical Intention." "Feed him only cereal," John said. We had been frantic that he would not get a balanced and nutritional meal. The idea sounded crazy!

We tried it. Tony loved it. However, after three or four meals, Missy got panicky. "Tony," she said, "Momma and Daddy are trying to poison you." We stopped. The contradiction was absurd.

It is an **anachronism** today. There was a time it was chic to blame your parents. Life is cruel. Disturbed persons are not unusual visitors to the cruel life. Some parents do not deserve to be parents. Difficult and disturbed people affect the lives of others—sometimes these people damage the lives of others.

Being Responsible

As unpleasant as it may sound, each person is individually responsible.

The Soul that Sins Will Die—Individual Responsibility (Ezek. 18:4)

" 'The fathers have eaten sour grapes, and the children's teeth are set on edge' " (Jer. 31:29). Parents may shape the personalities of children, but there will come a day of reckoning for both the parent and the child. Eventually, each person is responsible for himself or herself.

Parents can help children build for the future by giving time, dedication, and love. Or they can affect their future by denying these three.

Ultimately, the child must be responsible. A wonderful family lives with the history of a son who died of AIDS. They frequently think and sometimes ask: "Why?" and "What if?"

A good parent is one who lets the child forget it when a child makes a fool of himself or herself. Will the parent blame himself or herself for the child's foolishness?

The Soul that Is Righteous Will Surely Live (Ezek. 18:9)

Of course, righteousness is relative. It is hard to define. But, Ezekiel gives it a try in verses 5-8. A righteous person is honest, hard working, decent, keeps the Ten Commandments, and has integrity. These qualities may not help his children, but they provide a great role model.

Richard Foster wrote a wonderful book, *Celebration of Discipline: The Path to Spiritual Growth*. In his chapter on the discipline of submission he discusses the importance of self denial in the pilgrimage to spiritual growth. We are comfortable with "self-fulfillment" and self-actualization" but uncomfortable with self denial.[1] Self denial is not loss of identity or self hatred, or even self-contempt, but rather "The freedom to give way to others."[2] The best role model for **righteous** actions is building the freedom to give way to others. It is not the feeling of "All I do is for you" because that is passive aggression. It is simply "I am free to give you freedom."

Thomas á Kempis said, "to think always well and highly of others is great wisdom and perfection."[3]

Again we are back to **contradiction** and **paradox**. George Matheson said in a hymn,

> Make me a captive Lord and then
> I shall be free; force me to
> Render up my sword, and I shall
> Conqueror be. I sink in life's
> Alarms when by myself I stand;
> Imprison me within thine arms, and
> Strong shall be my hand.[4]

You will never think highly of yourself until you first think highly of others.

A Life-Style Can Be Changed (Ezek. 18:4-27)

The **key** word in individual responsibility is *accountability*. We are accountable to God. Children are accountable to parents and vice versa, but we are all accountable to God. It is a life-style, not an act. It can be **erased**.

" 'If anyone would come after me, he must deny himself and take up his cross and follow me" (Mark 8:34). Augustine said, "The confession of evil works is the first beginning of good works." **Erasure** begins with confession. It is completed by repentance. "If we confess our sins, he is faithful and just and will forgive us our sins . . . If we claim we have not sinned, we make him out to be a liar" (1 John 1:9-10).

You can change a life-style. The best choice is repentance and accountability to God. Ultimately God will judge (Ezek. 18:20).

A New Heart and Spirit Are the Only Hope (Ezek. 18:31)

The only way to deal with contradiction and paradox is with a new heart and spirit. Look at the Simpsons cartoon. America no longer watches the Anderson family of "Father Knows Best." America watches the Simpsons. The creators— Matt Groening, Jim Brooks, and Sam Simon—designed a parody of traditional sitcoms. It was an instant hit. Why? Adults like it because it is sophisticated satire. It helps us laugh at ourselves. A new heart and spirit are our only hope. Death is not the victor. Disease is not the ultimate foe.

Jim Brooks gave us "Taxi," *Terms of Endearment,* and "The Mary Tyler Moore Show." He gives us a counter-cultural shock. You can make a religion of parenting, but we all know it is unpredictable and fun with a new heart and spirit. A new heart and spirit puts a note of honesty back. Take the **contradiction**. It is absurd to think you will answer for your children's sins or vice versa. Only a new heart and spirit will suffice.

Notes

1. Richard Foster, *Celebration of Discipline: The Path to Spiritual Growth* (New York: Harper and Row, 1978), 99.
2. Ibid., 100.
3. Ibid.
4. George Matheson, *Hymns for Worship* (Nappanae, Ind.: Evangel Press, 1963), 248.

20

Discriminate Listening

"If only you would be altogether silent! For you that would be wisdom" (Job 13:5).

"Listening is the rude interruptions between my exclamations."

"Listening is the hardest work I do in communication."

In an article "The Three Faces of Love," Robert J. Trotter suggested a three-sided theory of love: commitment, intimacy, and passion.[1] None of these are possible without learning to listen to your mate. All involve "hearing" the needs of another. What keeps us from listening?

Filters are one reason. Personal concerns cause filters which preclude listening. Before listening is possible, there are filters to go through.

Preoccupation is a second reason.

Child: Mommy, can I spend the night with Gina?
Parent: Go brush your teeth.
Husband: Honey, I'm playing golf on Tuesday.
Wife: Did you remember to go to the cleaners?

I am preoccupied with pleasing my spouse. I can't hear obstacles. Listening takes concentration. Listening is the patience to wait without fretting, especially on the telephone. A teenager and her mother were visiting a neighbor. The neighbor said, "She's well-behaved."

"Not really, she's just not used to talking until she hears a dial tone," the mother said.

Some Aspects of Discriminate Listening

Believe in the value of what you have to share (Luke 8:16). After lighting a lamp, no one covers it over with a container." You are important. What you think is worth sharing. It is worth hearing. But also, give those rights to others. They are worth hearing.

Don't be boring. In order that those who come in may see the light, don't be boring. When you talk about yourself inordinately, it is a slow trip for a listener. Share what is interesting. Share not only what makes you look *good* but what makes you look *funny.*

An article in *Bits and Pieces* is on "Good Listeners." Some suggestions are:

• Look the speaker in the eye.

• Be attentive—don't roll your eyes or grimace when you hear something you don't agree with.

• Don't interrupt—try phrases like "go on . . ." or "I see . . ." instead of "now that reminds me . . ."

• Tell them what you think you heard. "Let me see if I understand."

• Consider carefully how you listen. "Therefore, consider carefully how you listen" (v. 18).[2]

"The Lord knows the thoughts of man" (Ps. 94:11). *Listen* to some biblical advice about listening:

• "He who has ears, let him hear" (Matt. 11:15).

• "The reason you do not hear is that you do not belong to God" (John 8:47). Now that one is tough.

• "For the time will come when men will not put up with sound doctrine. Instead, to suit their own desires, they will gather around them a great number of teachers to say what their itching ears want to hear" (2 Tim. 4:3).

• "A wise man listens to advice" (Prov. 12:15).

• "He who answers before listening—that is his folly and his shame" (Prov. 18:13).

Therefore, listen before answering (Prov. 18:13).

Listen to Others

(1) It tells them they're important.

(2) It compliments their contributions.

(3) It lifts their spirits.

(4) It encourages others to think.

(5) It increases your own value to them.

How to Listen

Listen to melodies not words. "The heart of the discerning acquires knowledge; the ears of the wise seek it out" (Prov. 18:15). Listen to inflections. They are clues to: joy, disappointment, anger, and warmth. Consider "I love you" as reassurance, then as warmth of affection.

*Listen with your **ears** and discipline your **tongue**.* "The tongue has the power of life and death" (Prov. 18:21).

Listen without filtering. "Listen to **advice and accept instruction**" (Prov. 19:20). Some people listen with a "Yes, but . . ." attitude. Don't rationalize. Don't rebuke. Accept good advice. That is how we grow. Prejudices, assumptions, and mind-sets are some of the filters.

Listen without judging. "He who guards his mouth and his tongue keeps himself from calamity" (Prov. 21:23). Oh, some may say this, but Proverbs also says, "Better to live in a desert than with a quarrelsome and ill-tempered wife" (21:19). It also says, "He who pursues righteousness and love finds life, prosperity and honor" (v. 21). So listen while you pursue righteousness and listen without judging.

"**Listen,** my son, and be wise, and keep your heart on the right path" (23:19).

*Listening must not be a **springboard for self-indulgence**.* Listening is not the penance you pay for the privilege of speech. It is a well-spring of affirmation to others.

Listening is a model of Christ and should be viewed as such. Open your hearts to revelation. "Whoever has will be given more; whoever does not have even what he thinks he has will be taken from him (Luke 8:18). " 'Though seeing, they may not see; though hearing, they may not understand' " (Luke 8:10). *Listening,* as a model of Christ, means loving and caring even in confusion.

Listen to God instead of instructing Him. Don't share it as an "exclusive" in the language of Zion.

Notes

1. Robert J. Trotter, "The Three Faces of Love," *Psychology Today,* September 1986.

2. "Good Listeners," *Bits and Pieces,* February 1990.

21

Elijah Had Warts

"And when he saw that, he arose, and ran for his life"
(1 Kings 19:3, author).

"A man may be a fool and not know it, but not if he is
married."

For the past nine months, I have had to deal with Planter's warts. They are painful, pernicious, and persistent. They are inconvenient, insidious, and inescapable. I told my podiatrist that I expected him to do something about them. He laughed and said if he could he would no longer have to work. I was not amused.

Warts are unpleasant and unsightly. They are a viral infection. The only cure is to wait until the body builds an immunity.

Elijah was a courageous hero. He made his stand against impossible odds. However, Jezebel did him in. He ran for his life. Elijah had warts, too.

Elijah Had Warts

Elijah Was a Cry Baby

" 'I am the only one left, and now they are trying to kill me too' " (1 Kings 19:10). We often feel the pain of being alone. We feel we are the only one who cares about the welfare of the church. We are the only one concerned about reaching the lost, growing the disciples, and feeding the sheep. We cry, too!

Elijah Was Self-Indulgent

"And he said, 'Do it a third time,' and they did it a third time" (1 Kings 18:34, NASB). Once would have been enough. He had asked them to fill four barrels with water and pour it on the burnt sacrifice and wood. He wanted to show them up. He wanted blood. We, too, are often self-indulgent. It is not enough to win. We want to rub it in.

Elijah Was a Quitter

"He requested for himself that he might die, and said, 'It is enough; now, O Lord, take my life'" (1 Kings 19:4, NASB).

The best time to write a letter of resignation is Monday morning after a disappointing Sunday. What minister has not considered quitting on Monday morning? Some do quit. The ranks of stock brokers, management consultants, communication experts, and teachers are now filled with ex-preachers.

A friend of mine said of the ministry: "The pay isn't so hot, but you can't beat the retirement plan." That is little consolation when you have the "blahs and blues" and the prospects don't look any better.

Elijah Milked the Accolades

"And he said to him, 'Go back again, for what have I done to you?'" (1 Kings 19:20, NASB). The conversation was with his disciple Elisha. Elijah had already thrown his cloak around him. He had "claimed" him as a disciple. When Elisha told him how wonderful he was, "Let me, I pray thee, kiss my father and my mother, and then I will follow thee" (1 Kings 19:20, KJV). Elijah came back with "My goodness, what have I done?" Now, he knew exactly what he had done. He was milking the accolades from Elisha.

To be complimented for what a wonderful job we are doing, ministers have to "position" ourselves to get the accolades. As I was preparing this devotional, I accidentally typed the word *poison* ourselves, instead of *position* ourselves. It still works, doesn't it?

Elijah Had Pizzazz

I don't know how to describe or define pizzazz. I know it when I see it. Elijah had pizzazz. It has to do with "class."

Last week the Miracles, a group of mentally retarded adults, sang in a chapel service I attended. Each adult was asked to introduce himself or herself. Each person spoke softly. Then, one young man with some distorted features virtually exploded with his introduction. It was unlike any of the others. "I'm John Hughes. I work in maintenance." The awkwardness of the moment could have caused nervous laughter, but not the slightest snigger was heard. The people felt his personality and accepted him. That is class. I cannot define it, but I know it when I see it.

A woman had developed Alzheimer's disease. Her husband of fifty-two years talked with the reporter beside her hospital bed. She did not recognize him.

"That's OK," he said. "She took care of me when I needed it. I'll take care of her. She's my sweetheart." He reached down and kissed her gnarled and distorted face. I cried.

Today the topic of conversation among growing churches is, "Does the preacher have pizzazz?" If not, it is presumed that the church will not grow. It helps, but growth is not dependent on "pizzazz." It is, however, dependent on dedication and commitment.

• *Fed by the birds*. The ravens brought him bread and meat in the morning" (1 Kings 17:6, NASB). Now, does that have pizzazz or what?

• *A bottomless jar of flour and jug of oil*. He had the touch of blessing to the widow at Zarephath. " 'The jar of flour will not be used up and the jug of oil will not run dry until the day the Lord gives rain on the land' " (1 Kings 17:14).

When he was fed by the birds, it showed God loved him. When he fed the widow, it showed he loved others. That is the way it works with pizzazz. You want to be able to be a blessing to others; recognize the blessing of God to you.

• *Not afraid of the odds*. "I am the only one of the Lord's prophets left, but Baal has four hundred and fifty prophets" (1 Kings 18:22). However, he was not afraid of the odds. If God is on your side, you have a majority.

• *Called a spade, a spade*. He told it like it was. He may have been the Howard Cosell of prophecy. " 'How long will you waver between two opinions? If the Lord is God, follow him; but if Baal is God, follow him" (1 Kings 18:21).

Telling it like it is and Telling it like you think it is may be entirely different. We must know the difference in conviction and prejudice when we speak of "we and they" preaching because it is dangerous. If you tell your brother he is wrong, you better do it to help him and not simply to prove your own point. Otherwise, it is "contentious."

Elijah was calling the people back to God. He said, You have pussyfooted around long enough. Get off the fence. Call in the cows. It's time to milk and feed the cattle.

• *A cynic with a cause*. There is no way to ignore these people. " 'Shout louder!' he said, 'Surely he is a god! Perhaps he is deep in thought, or busy, or traveling. Maybe he is sleeping and must be awakened' " (1 Kings 18:27).

Elijah had a clear focus on the enemy. Cynics usually do. "If I have to do it myself, I'll do it."

• *Not afraid to get in the trenches*. " 'Come here to me. They came to him, and he repaired the altar of the Lord, which was in ruins" (1 Kings 18:30). Those with pizzazz are not afraid to get down and get dirty. They don't say, "Bring me a cup of coffee." They say, "Would you like a cup of coffee as I fix mine?"

• *Elijah was from Missouri, the "show me" state.* Elijah was waiting for the dramatic, but God speaks in His own way. God is wont to speak in unpredictable and unexpected ways. In 1 Kings 19, a wind tore the mountains apart and shattered the rocks, but God was not in the wind. There was an earthquake, but the Lord was not in the earthquake. There was a fire, but the Lord was not in the fire. After the fire came a gentle whisper. Elijah wanted to be shown dramatically, but God was there all the time.

• *Elijah Left a Legacy.* Anyone with pizzazz usually leaves a legacy. Elijah was taken up to heaven in a whirlwind. Elisha asked, " 'Let me inherit a double portion of your spirit' " (2 Kings 2:9). Elijah was reluctant, but he agreed. "The company of the prophets from Jericho, who were watching, said, 'The spirit of Elijah is resting on Elisha' " (2:15).

I may be remembered best by my warts. But, I hope I am remembered also by some pizzazz. Although some think my life is "for the birds," I hope I am fed by some birds. I do not have the gift of miracles as did Elijah, but I can create a bottomless jar of love and a bottomless jug of good will.

You and I do not have to beat the odds, but we need not fear them either. The courage to call a spade a spade should be our signature. If I am a cynic, let it be for the cause of Christ and not personal vendettas. The real work is in the trenches. To win people to Christ, we must get in the trenches with them.

The fact that I am from Missouri should not blind me to God acting in the unexpected. God does not have to "show me."

I wish my legacy could be: "He helped others solve their problems." Then I would give a double portion of my spirit to at least one. Do you have an Elisha?

22

Bathing in Baloney

"Actors tend to bathe in baloney."[1]

"So the man went and washed, and came home seeing" (John 9:7).

One reason the church is incredible to many is that Christians sometimes bathe in baloney.

A prominent person spoke in our chapel services, which start at 7:30 a.m. and conclude at 8:00 a.m. Almost all speakers honor the time frame.

"I was encouraged to stop on time," he laughed. "I shall do that." However, enamored with the sound of his own voice, he could not quit. He spoke until all were nervous with the anxiety of embarrassment for him—*bathed in baloney*.

Richard Berendzen, former American University president, received a suspended sentence after extended therapy. He had made obscene phone calls to Susan Allen. His behavior was "triggered" at his father's funeral (who died in the room where he was abused as a child). Berendzen's apology was not enough. Allen said, "They know that what they're doing is wrong. They can choose to continue or they can choose to say, 'That's it. . . .'"[2]

The idea "I can't stop myself" is bathed in baloney. It avoids the question of responsibility. An alcoholic says, "I'm not hurting anyone but myself." But what about the spouse, children, friends, and parents? What about embarrassment to those who care? Of course, they're ill and addicted. "I can't help myself" is a feeble plea for asking family and friends to "wink" at the gravity of the situation.

June Carter Cash in describing her relationship with her husband, Johnny, and his problem with drugs said there comes a time when those who care must say stop. The idea that this person can continue to get away with this absurdity of behavior is bathed in baloney.

The Bible Story (John 9:1-41)

" 'So I went and washed, and then I could see.' " Jesus made mud. Rubbed it on the blind man's eyes. He told him to wash in the pool of Siloam. He came back seeing. The Pharisees' response was baloney! They tried to explain away the miracle:

(1) He could see already. It was a hoax.

(2) It's a different person. He is not the one. He just looks like him (v. 8).

(3) He would know *where* the man was who healed him. He doesn't know (v. 12).

(4) It was of the devil, not God (v. 16).

(5) His parents couldn't back up his story (v. 20*ff*).

Like the Pharisees, we find it difficult to be trusting. Sometimes our clichés give us reason to be skeptical:

(1) "The check's in the mail." Sure it is.

(2) "You can trust me." Never trust a broadly grinning car salesman who implores, "Trust me."

(3) "I love everybody." It's hollow optimism.

(4) "This is the first day of the rest of your life." That's empty hope! I want my funeral epitaph to read "This is the last day of the rest of my life." That's hope!

(5) "God will take care of you." It's ambiguous spiritual comfort. Convince me of the fact with actions, not spiritual clichés.

(6) "I'm OK; You're OK." Thomas Harris said it. It's self-indulgent irresponsibility. None of us are OK without Christ, but the phrase sold books.

(7) "Let's have lunch." Or, "Keep in touch." Either way, we don't really mean what we say.

Some ministerial statements have been known to bathe in baloney.

(1) "Good to see you." Translation: I can't remember your name.

(2) "Where are you now?" Translation: Let's compare churches.

(3) "These are the greatest people on earth." Translation: They raised my salary.

(4) This is the best church I've ever had." Translation: I can't get another one now.

(5) "I've never been happier." Translation: You should've seen my last church.

(6) "I'm walking on air. I'm so happy." Translation: One person called to tell me how she appreciated my sermon.

Here are ways to slice the baloney to make it edible and credible:

- Respect the listener (John 9:31).
- Learn from anyone (John 9:34).
- Don't be deterred by doubters (John 9:39).
- Recognize spiritual impoverishment (John 9:40).
- Be credible (John 10:1). I am telling you the truth.
- The truth is tragic.

Frederick Buechner, in *Telling the Truth,* records the story of Henry Ward Beecher traveling to Yale in January 31, 1872, to deliver the Beecher lectures named after his father. He struggled in preparation. He was facing a lawsuit for adultery with one of his parishioners. He was shaving at 2:00 in the morning. He stared at his *shame* and *horror*. He cut himself and, melodramatically, wrote those lectures in blood to symbolize his own folly. He felt that God would be merciful if he confessed and faced his sins with repentance. Beecher felt he was never more credible and real than in those lectures. His *humanity* made him credible—no longer bathed in baloney.

In *King Lear,* Gloucester had to have his eyes put out before he could see the truth about himself and his sons. His recognition of his own *depravity* made him credible—no longer bathed in baloney. Lear lost his crown and kingdom because of his evil daughters. Then he became king for the first time.

Edgar, Gloucester's son, has the closing line, as he is surrounded by dead bodies.

> "The weight of this sad time we must obey
> "Speak what we *feel,* not what we *ought to say.*"[3]

" 'I hate, I despise your religious feasts; I cannot stand your assemblies. But let justice roll on like a river, righteousness like a never-failing stream!" (Amos 5:21,24).

The ones who are bathed in baloney may be close to the yiddish word *schlemiel,* which is a kind of person who spills soup on people. *Schlemozzle* is the one the soup is spilled on. If we are bathed in baloney (by the schlemiel) we deserve the name *schlemozzle.* Stephen Crane's poem says:

> A man said to the universe
> "Sir I exist!"
> "However," replied the universe
> "The fact has not created in me
> A sense of obligation."

The world doesn't owe us (baloney); we owe the world (reality). Albert Carmus in "Doctrine of the Absurd" said, "Man wants life to make sense. Life has an inexorable refusal to do so."

Baloney is the assertion that life makes sense. Reality is knowing only God can make sense of life. Baloney is theorizing about the Christian life. Reality is living the Beatitudes and the Sermon on the Mount daily. Baloney is claiming our own knowledge and power. Reality is living with confusion and trusting God. Baloney is blindness to wonder, awe, and miracles. Reality is seeing the beauty of God in the commonplace and predictable.

How can *Donald Duck* be flattened by a stream roller in one scene and fully put together in another? It is baloney. It is the "miracle" of the hand of the cartoonist. It is also poetic license. How can a person be flattened by sin on the one hand and redeemed in the next breath? It is the *miracle* of the hand of God. It is incredible to humans, but God can do it!

Conclusion

A bird does not *sing* because it has an answer but because it has a song. To feel we have answers to all questions asked in the Christian life is *baloney;* to know we have access to the One with answers is a song.

Fury in Christianity is often just that. Truth, honesty, integrity, and love are not baloney. These are ingredients with which we build our lives.

Notes

1. Paul Newman's commencement speech at Sarah Lawrence College, Bronxville, New York, where his wife, JoAnne Woodward, and daughter, Clea, received bachelor degrees.
2. *Newsweek,* June 11, 1990, 55.
3. William Shakespeare, *King Lear,* 5.3.324-25.

23

My Dad Was a Pistol, Too

"God Himself will provide" (Gen. 22:8).

"He brought life to wherever he happened to be."[1]

A father can set you free—Ishmael (Gen. 21:14). A father can tie you down—Isaac (Gen. 22:9). The prodigal son story (Luke 15:11-32) is remarkable. It has three dimensions, and it develops from three angles. It is a wonderful Father's Day story.

First, the prodigal brother had responsibility without freedom which is self-imposed slavery. He will both regret and resent it, and he did.

Second, the prodigal son had freedom without responsibility which led to rebellion and anarchy. The enemy is within. It is sin. He will grow to despise himself.

Third, the prodigal father had freedom with responsibility. He loved both his sons. He set them both free. Neither was ready. That is *grace*. He let them make their own mistakes. The father's work is giving a child enough freedom to make mistakes and enough grace to take them back when the child makes them.

Do you have good memories of your dad? I do! If Dad said, "Get up, we're wasting daylight," we got up. He meant now, not ten minutes from now.

If he said, "It's going to rain," while the sun was shining and not a cloud in the sky, we rejoiced. Why? We didn't work in the cotton and corn when it rained. Dad knew what he was talking about. We trusted him.

If he said, "I'm disappointed in you," as he did when I lied about buying a walkie-talkie with money I had stolen from him, I died a thousand deaths. I forgot the whipping but remember that phrase.

If he said, "I'm proud of you," as he did when he found out I was valedictorian, it was much sweeter to hear his words than the words of the announcement in the student body awards.

He once told me affectionately he envied me. I did not understand, but I knew it was a gesture of love. He was *poor,* but he was never *pitiful.* When a crop failed, he would grieve, but he did not blame. All six of us children felt we were Dad's "favorite." He was a poor money manager, but we had little money to manage.

He often attended my basketball games, but he watched from the door. He walked in and out during the game. He once told me he could not stand to see me get fouled. This is the same man who made me work a ten-hour day hoeing cotton in 100-degree weather at age eight. It was not a contradiction to him. Basketball was a *game.* Work was *survival.* If you suffer pain, it should be for survival, not for a game.

A Father's Love Is Confusing

Abraham was the father of Ishmael. Hagar was Ishmael's mother. Sarah had been barren. At age ninety, Sarah gave birth to Isaac. Abraham was a hundred.

Sarah gave Hagar her marching orders to protect Isaac's territory. "Abraham sent her off with the boy" (Gen. 21:14). This was after the writer of Genesis concluded, "The matter distressed Abraham greatly because it concerned his son" (21:11). Even in his humanity, he had faith. "God was with the boy as he grew up" (v. 20). Later his faith would be tested. "Take your son . . . sacrifice him" (22:2).

"I'm doing what's best for you." You did not believe it when your dad said it. You do now and so do I. "This will hurt me more than it hurts you." You did not believe it when he said it. You do now and so do I. "I have great confidence in you." It came soon after he was disappointed in me. I did not believe it when he said it. I do now. Did Isaac believe "God himself will provide" (22:8)? A father's love is confusing.

A Father's Love Needs Direction

It is too easy to allow sentimentality to consume us. We forget a father's love needs direction, too. God said to Abraham, "Do not be distressed about the boy."

Lewis Grizzard wrote about his father in *My Daddy Was a Pistol and I'm a Son of a Gun.* His father was a drunk, a lovable drunk, but a drunk nevertheless. "They say my daddy spoiled me from the very first day. 'You weren't three weeks old and he had you on his lap while he was coaching a basketball game.'"[2] Grizzard's father and mother divorced. His grandparents raised him from age six. His father was a con man. He would move into a small town, go to a church, sit up front so he could be heard, and stake a claim to the words "that fine looking gentleman with the grey hair and beautiful voice." He would borrow large sums of money from casual friends. Lewis Grizzard loved him—even though he needed direction.

He and his stepbrother, Ludlow Porch, a radio talk-show host in Atlanta, commented after his death, "We could have set him up with a nice place to live, hire somebody to look after him, and *just enjoy* him."[3] Ludlow loved him, too.

God guided Abraham even in the midst of the selfish wishes of Sarah. Ishmael would start another nation. God is like that. He can take the sour of our selfishness and turn it into the sweetness of service to others.

Your father may not be perfect, but he's the only one you have. Trust God to give him direction.

A Father's Love Is Never Finished

"Where is the lamb?" asked Isaac (22:7).

"God himself will provide the lamb" (v. 8). They even named the place *Jahweh Jireh* (God will provide). The situation was "superdrama." God said to Abraham, "I will make you into a great nation and I will bless you; I will make your name great, and you will be a blessing" (12:2). That is the tenderest, most permanent part of Abraham's love; it was never finished. It just kept growing. He had been blessed so he blessed others. Let us recapture that blessing from a Father that Abraham modeled.

A Father's Family Devotion Is to His Wife First

It "distressed" him, but he sent his handmaiden and son packing. Hagar and Ishmael were second to Sarah. A father should be devoted to his children, but he should be more devoted to his wife.

A Father's Love Is Indiscriminate and Permanent, Even Though Often Tested

Fathers and grandfathers will appreciate this story. A four-year-old girl was describing a beautiful sunset to her mother. "And God painted it left-handed," she said.

The mother was confused, "Why left-handed?"

"Because Jesus was sitting on his right hand," she said.

Isn't it great to love your child? It's easy to love them when they're cute. A father loves when they come in drunk or are jailed. He loves when they disobey or fail a course. He loves when they are arrogant or impudent. He corrects. He is disappointed. He loves.

A Father's Love Is Not Perfect

Abraham rejected one. He was about to abandon another, but he learned his lesson.

A parrot was bought by a church woman. The parrot had been taught foul language, and his new owner felt she could correct him. Sure enough, on the first day, he let out a loud oath. The church woman had just the solution. "I told you not to say that," she said and put him in the freezer for two hours.

Two hours later, the repentant parrot came out shivering. "I want to re-dedicate my life," he said, "but tell me one thing. If I got two hours in the freezer for cussing, what horrible thing did that turkey I saw in there do?"

A parrot learned his lesson. Fathers do, too. We keep trying until we get it right.

He gives fathers a second chance to get it right. God knows we're turkeys, but He treats us more like parrots. He puts us in the freezer, but He takes us out because He loves us.

Some Lessons for Fathers

(1) A father's first loyalty is to God.

(2) A father's next loyalty is to his wife, not his children.

(3) A father should not sweat the small squabbles if he is to be respected in the big squabbles. (See Gen. 20:9-11.)

(4) A concession is made for a purpose.

(5) The biggest blessings follow the biggest sacrifices. (See Gen. 22:16-17.)

(6) When you least expect it, God will provide. (See Gen. 22:13-14.)

Notes

1. Lewis Grizzard, *My Daddy Was a Pistol and I'm a Son of a Gun* (New York: Villard Books, 1986), 265.

2. Ibid., 74.

3. Ibid., 280.

24

Small Sheep Make Cranky Shepherds

"You who turn justice into bitterness and cast righteousness to the ground" (Amos 5:7).

"An optimist will let a child take a new car on a date; A pessimist won't; A cynic did."

Amos was a sheepherder from Tekoa. Some Old Testament scholars think he tended a special species of dwarfed sheep called nakav. These sheep were small perhaps 12 to 18 inches tall, and may be the same kind of sheep Amos tended. In 2 Kings 3:4, we find King Mesha, the king of Moab, was a breeder of dwarfed sheep. Sheep are hard to take care of. The abundance of wool from ordinary sheep makes shepherding worthwhile, but a dwarfed sheep takes an abundance of energy and toil with minimum results. Also, they could be hard to find.

I'm not sure that was why Amos was cranky, but all you have to do is read the Book of Amos, and you know that he was cranky. Listen to what he says, "They sell the righteous for silver, and the needy for a pair of sandals" (Amos 2:6). "They trample on the heads of the poor" (2:7). "They do not know how to do right" (3:10). "Hear this word, you cows of Bashan" (4:1). "You turn justice into bitterness and cast righteousness to the ground" (5:7). He was cranky, but he had a cause.

Nelson Mandela, the champion of the abolition of apartheid, talked to Ted Coppell on June 21, 1990. When Coppell suggested the South African government had reported that they were making strides to abolish apartheid, Mandela did not respond with words; he laughed. It was not a laughter of joy. It was a laughter of cyncism. Like a spider drawing the fly into the web, Mandela brought the heretofore self-confident Coppell into the drama of historical intrusion of righteousness. At one point, Coppell did not respond to Mandela when he said, "Have I paralyzed you?" Righteousness rolled on like a never-failing stream. Justice poured through like a river. They broke for a commercial.

When people have a cause, they may appear to be cranky. More likely, they are single-minded with purpose. Amos was single-minded with purpose. Dwarfed sheep or not!

Some feel Amos was a shepherd of the temple flocks. If that was true, he was close to the religious action. He knew hypocrisy when he saw it. He knew the people who wanted to be religious but did not have the resources.

Amos was not of religious breeding. "'I was neither a prophet nor a prophet's son, but I was a shepherd, and I also took care of sycamore-fig trees. But the Lord took me from tending the flock and said to me, "Go, prophesy to my people Israel."'" (7:14-15).

Some of the worst enemies of the church are within. Why? Unfortunately, "familiarity breeds contempt." Some persons can not deal with the fact that ministers are people with faults and weaknesses. They appear to be so human that they could not possibly represent the divine. Disillusioned persons often come from within the church, and it makes them testy, cranky, and certainly hard to get along with.

Amos felt that the standard of justice should be more than an ethical code. He felt it should be right actions. He saw just the opposite. Amos was a simple, straightforward shepherd. The way he saw it, a person should have a knowledge of God first, and then act rightly. We are no different. Those who know God should act like it.

What made Amos cranky? Was it little sheep or little people? Was it dwarfed animals or dwarfed morality? Was it miniature show-sheep with little wool? Or, was it miniature show-priests with little religion? Something made him cranky and perhaps cynical but certainly rightfully so. "They sell the righteous for silver, and the needy for a pair of sandals" (2:6). Justice has been denied *because* the people are poor and needy. You trample upon the poor (5:11), but your day is coming.

Small Churches Make Ministers Cranky

Some ministers with lofty ideals and self-indulgent notions about their abilities crave large churches and resent the churches they are in. On a higher level, some ministers with a sense of justice and righteousness resent the "small" churches with limited visions and drowned-out dreams. They resent the mentality of "getting by." They resent the idea that some people are "not our kind of folks." They resent the bickering, gossip, and apathy. In short, some churches are small because of their numbers; some churches are small because of their behavior. I have little regard for the ministers who resent their churches because of their numbers. I respect the ministers who are cranky because of small behavior.

A minister was complaining to his colleague about his batting average in getting some of his ideas about church growth adopted. The colleague reminded him that Ty Cobb, the best hitter in baseball, averaged only .367. That means he got one hit about every third time at bat. The rejection of two out of three of a minister's ideas does not make the church small. The reality is that frequently two out of three of the minister's ideas are bad. Rejection of ideas does not make the church small. However, rejection of justice and righteousness does make the church small.

When It Is Not OK for the Shepherd to Be Cranky

When the sheep are small and it affects marketability. Smallness in behavior affects marketability with bickering, complaining, and backbiting.

Churches look at ministers who are marketable. If large churches have popular ministers, other churches are usually interested. They want them for their own.

The trap is in seeing small as being insignificant. Most churches have fewer than three hundred members. To the mega-church that is small. However, some of the best preachers I have heard are in those "small" churches.

It is not OK for the shepherd to be cranky if he is convinced he is stuck in a "one-horse-town" church.

"My work is finished here" is the cry of a person who has become cranky because he has lost his vision. A minister's work is never finished where people congregate.

When the shepherd's staff is a rod, anger is disguised as prophecy. Some ministers give signals of being an accident looking for a place to happen. We have no way of knowing how much anger has been disguised as prophecy. At the very best, anger can be masked as concern.

It's one thing to step on church member's toes. It is quite another to step on their hearts and take away their dignity, and feelings of self-worth. A rod has no place with those who love.

When the shepherd does not mourn the loss of sheep. Amos warned the people, but he felt for their travail. The shepherd that does not mourn the loss of sheep is no longer a shepherd. A minister that does not mourn the inactive church member is no longer a minister.

When It Is OK for the Shepherd to Be Cranky

When there is a false sense of security. A church should be uncomfortable if it is to be effective: It should not be comfortable. A ship may be beautiful docked, but that is not what a ship is for. A church should be uncomfortable with injustice, unrighteousness, lying, stealing, thievery, and idolatry. When there is no sense of discomfort, a church will shrivel and die. Be grateful for the cantankerous. They keep you on your toes. Be cranky with a false sense of security. A church is about reaching people. Comfort is about being satisfied with the people already reached.

When there is inhumane treatment of humankind. A church should be concerned about the abolition of apartheid, about the homeless, about the hungry, and about the mistreatment of children. These are reasons to be cranky. Amos was. We should, too.

When people use other people for their own gain. Some people are friendly if it is profitable. Some are religious if it benefits them. Amos gets serious with those "who trample the needy and do away with the poor" (8:4). If people are being used, the prophet should be cranky with those who are using them.

George Burns sang about two kinds of people. Those who love things and use people to get them and those who love people and use things to show them.

The worst kind of idolatry is to treat people with no respect. It shows affection for things and not persons. The worst kind of idolatry is to desire a house and furnishings more than you desire the friendship of persons who have given a part of themselves to you.

When repentance is missing. "'The days are coming, . . . when the reaper will be overtaken by the plowman and the planter by the one treading grapes. New wine will drip from the mountains and flow from all the hills'" (9:13). How? Through repentance; "Seek me and live" (5:6). "Let justice roll on like a river, righteousness like a never-failing stream!" (5:24). Repentance takes the crankiness out of everyone.

Small sheep make cranky shepherds. Some crankiness is legitimate. It has reconciliation as a motive. However, some doesn't. We need to examine our crankiness regularly.

Some Signs of a Cranky Shepherd

(1) "I never get a break." A lot of people are waiting to win the *Reader's Digest* Sweepstakes.

(2) "I deserve it." Patrick Henry said, "Give me liberty or give me death." The next generation shouted, "Give me liberty." Our generation shouts, "Give me."

(3) "I need my space." That's the Garfield generation.

(4) "I'm doing the best I can." Don't push me.

(5) "Everything happens to me." That's the Ziggy complex. A friend of mine made a hole-in-one. The problem was the first ball he hit on the par three went into the water. His score for the hole was three.

(6) "Get off my case." Give me a break. I don't want to be accountable, just free.

(7) "I say what I feel." Unbridled candor is a luxury of irresponsibility. Some people are like buttons: They pop off at the wrong time.

How to Avoid Crankiness

(1) "Take a shower." Get ready for the day of troubles or turmoil. Some church members are neatly starched and ironed, but they have never been washed.

(2) "Get out of a rut and on the right track." When you're in a rut, you get bored. Even when you are on the track, you can get run over if you just sit there so get on the right track. Arrange your mental outlook.

(3) "Give others room to be wrong." You don't have to correct every error. Some people want to take up the dirty dishes before people are through eating. It will wait.

(4) "Eat some prunes." They are full of iron. They cleanse the soul. They help you avoid being cranky.

(5) "Consider the planted seed." You can't see it, but you know it's growing. Comfort comes from helping yourself remember the hope of promises to come.

(6) "Consider the uniqueness." Dwarfed sheep are unlike any other breed. You are also unlike anyone else.

(7) "Take another route." Eat at another restaurant. Sit at a different seat. In others words, change your routine.

(8) "God cares." God is too kind to do anything cruel, too wise to make a mistake, and too deep to explain Himself. God cares even when it seems He doesn't.

25

When Bad Things Happen to Good People

"I have to believe that everything that happens in life, happens for a purpose. Somehow or other, everything that happens to us is meant for our good."[1]

"How great are your works, O Lord, how profound your thoughts! The senseless man does not know, fools do not understand" (Ps. 92:5-6).

A child was taken from us by an unmanageable disease. The anguish is also unmanageable. Many have confronted unanswerable questions about life and death, pain and suffering.

A second sister from a family was taken within days. This family is dealing with life and death issues. Others in our family have faced ultimate dilemmas about death and vocation. A friend of mine lies dying yet has a hope that would baffle the strongest of the theologians. He is young, intelligent, and productive.

My daughter, granddaughter, and I visited my sister in Chattanooga this past July 4. My sister and brother-in-law are legally blind. Their two mentally retarded children, ages fifty-one and forty-five, are also blind. She is also afflicted with crippling arthritis. Some of their biggest problems are how to manage to get groceries from the store and to the doctor. She said occasionally things get a little tough.

"When my heart was grieved and my spirit embittered, I was senseless and ignorant; I was a brute beast before you. Yet I am always with you. My flesh and my heart never fail, but God is the strength of my heart and my portion" (Ps. 73:21-23,26). A few days ago I conducted a funeral for Todd and Terry Thompson who lost an infant daughter. It is impossible to be convincing in comfort. The universal question is: Why me, Lord?" Harold Kushner tried to give a helpful response but not an answer in his work *When Bad Things Happen to Good People.*

Some Questions Have No Answers

To understand why each heart needs strength and bad things happen to good people, we begin with a premise: *some questions have no answers.* Life is not connected. Life is not a tapestry of woven ideas that can be explained. If it were, life would not be confusing. God would not be needed. People could explain the confusions of life, and we would eventually be microcosms of God. We would not need God. Some questions have no answers, and we do need God.

In Thornton Wilder's, *The Bridge of San Luis Rey,* a rope bridge breaks over a chasm, and five people who are crossing the bridge fall to their deaths. A young priest, troubled by the event, comes to an enigmatic conclusion: All five had recently resolved a problematic situation in their lives and were now about to enter a new phase. *Death was appropriate,* thinks the priest. He was wrong. Some questions have no answers.

Forty years later, Wilder wrote *The Eighth Day.* A family is ruined by bad luck and hostility. The man was a good and decent man, but there is no happy ending. Instead Wilder offers a beautiful tapestry. On one side it is an intricately woven work of art, drawing together threads of different lengths and colors to make up an inspiring picture. However, turn it over and it is a hodgepodge of many threads—some short and some long . . . going in all directions. The conclusion is God has a pattern into which all of our lives fit. Some lives are twisted, knotted, or cut short; it appears there is no pattern. God's pattern of reward and punishment seems arbitrary and without design. Looked at from the other side, from God's vantage point, every twist and knot is seen to have its place in a great design that adds up to a work of art.

Some deal with suffering as does the Talmud (written between 200 B.C. and A.D. 500). If you go to the marketplace, you will see the potter hitting his clay pots with a stick to show how strong and solid they are. The wise potter hits only the strongest pots, never the flawed ones. God sends such tests and afflictions to people He knows are capable of handling them. That is sheer folly. I have seen people buckle and become mentally anguished because of pain and bad things happening to them. A hundred thousand unsuspecting families a year have handicapped children born to them. Some are certainly not capable of dealing with the clamor of invasion into their peaceful lives. God doesn't "zap" people indiscriminately.

Kushner lost his son Aaron at age fifteen with the disease *progeria.* He, like writer Harriet Sarnoff Schiff in the book *The Bereaved Parent,* could not accept the well-intentioned words of the clergyman: "I know that God only let this happen to you because He knows that you are strong enough to handle it." Schiff says her reaction was, "If only I were a weaker person, Robbie would still be alive." *The clergyman's words do not answer the question.* Some questions have no answers.

All Events and Happenings Are Not Connected

"If I hadn't gone on vacation, we would not have had the wreck." "If we had just had the one child, she wouldn't have had the illness." "If I had been kinder, she wouldn't have died so soon." People look for connections. Action gets response. It is cause and effect, but some things have no connections. You can not live peaceably in this world until you can reconcile that fact.

"If I hadn't nagged, he wouldn't have left." "If I hadn't gotten so angry at her, she would not have died." Our guilt and our finite mind cause us to look for connections, especially in tragedy and suffering. The fact remains some events and happenings are not connected. "How great are your works, O Lord, how profound your thoughts! The senseless man does not know, fools do not understand" (Ps. 92:5-6). God does not make mistakes. *People just don't know how to solve God's profound drama of living.* "The Lord knows the thoughts of man; he knows that they are futile" (Ps. 94:11). People cannot *connect* and make sense out of God's universe.

Kushner concludes his thoughts on "unconnectedness" in the chapter "Sometimes There Is No Reason." At least there is no reason that people can conclude. We are not God. We can not *connect* God's thoughts and plans. It is that simple.

Brother Juniper in *The Bridge of San Luis Rey* says the tragedy happened because recently the five who were killed had "put things together," but some can not put things together.

Joseph Heller in *Catch 22* asked, "How much reverence can you have for a Supreme Being who finds it necessary to include tooth decay?" Some things are just not connected. Pain and misery are a part of life. Why? There are no answers. There is no connection.

How many innocent people died who were a part of the six million of the Holocaust? Why? Because Hitler was a demented evil genius who was joined by thousands in his madness. However, that is not the complete answer. There is no complete answer.

An old Iranian folk proverb says, "If you see a blind man, kick him; why should you be kinder than God?" The implication is God punishes with affliction and misery—no He doesn't! Do you see the improbable logic in that twisted proverb? After He healed a man born blind, Jesus told the Pharisees, "Neither this man nor his parents sinned" (John 9:3). It was to fulfill the works of God. God's works aren't always connected for us to understand.

People Cannot Blame Themselves

God will help those who stop hurting themselves. Part of our difficulty comes because we have a need to believe that the world makes sense, and there is a cause for every effect and a reason for everything that happens. The second part of our trouble is the notion that we are the cause of what happens, especially the bad things that happen.

"Step on a crack, break your grandmother's back." We play games with ourselves. What did I do wrong? Where did I fail? Why is God doing this to me? We make ourselves the center of the universe, as if God singled us out to be the cause of disaster. God can not start helping us until we stop hurting ourselves.

We must move from self-pity to self-preservation. How? By proclaiming, "'The Lord is upright; he is my Rock, and there is no wickedness in him" (Ps. 92:15).

An alcoholic son cannot lay the blame at the door of parents. A cancerous wife cannot lay the blame at the door of a husband. A tragic rape victim cannot lay the blame at the door of society. There is evil in this world—both natural and personal. We must deal with it. The devil is alive and well, not the result of maladjusted behavior.

The Real Question: What Am I Going to Do About It?

Here is the most predictable question: Why did this happen to me? What did I do to deserve this? Here is the question that shows faith in God: Now that this has happened to me, what am I going to do about it?

Who does suffering serve? Dorothee Soelle, a German theologian, speaks of the "devil's martyrs." She says those who force themselves into despair and disbelief are the devil's martyrs. "God's martyrs" are those who give suffering meaning, allow illness room to exist, see accidents as a fact of life, and view human tragedy as inevitable.

Remember more good than bad things happen. Life's disasters are upsetting, but they are exceptional. Most illnesses are curable. Most airplanes take off and land safely. The rapist, robber, and inoperable tumor are life-shattering exceptions, but they are exceptions. When you have been hurt by life, it may be hard to keep that in mind.

A nineteenth-century Hasidic rabbi put it, "Human beings are God's language." You can be a person of love; that is what you can do about it. You may be angry at the bad situation. It is natural. You may have feelings of despair. It is predictable. Anger at God is OK. He can take it. To answer the question: "What are you going to do about it?" you must involve yourself in loving others. That is the only cure. That is the only solace. That is the only comfort—involving yourself in the love of others. *That is what God did for you.*

Jack Riemer wrote in *Likrat Shabhbat,*

> We cannot merely pray to You, O God, to end war;
> For we know that You have made the world in a way
> That man must find his own path to peace
> Within himself and with his neighbor.
> We cannot merely pray to you O God to end despair,
> For you have already given us the power
> to clear away slums and to give hope
> if we would only use our power justly.
> We cannot merely pray to you O God to end disease,
> for you have already given us great minds with which
> to search out cures and healing,
> If we would only use them constructively.
> Therefore, we pray to you instead, O God . . . for strength,
> determination, and willpower, to Do instead of just to pray, to
> BECOME instead of merely to wish.[2]

Human Beings Are God's Language

This week on HBO in the program "Child of Rage" a six-year-old girl cold-heartedly attempted to murder her younger brother. She hid knives with the express purpose of killing her parents. Why? Some questions have no answers. Although therapists have done wonders in bringing her back to some form of conscience and civility, some events are not connected. The parents had the agony of guilt on their faces. Although the little girl had been abused and mistreated at an even earlier age by the natural parent, the adoptive parents seemed to assume some of the guilt, but people cannot blame themselves for unstructured tragedy and suffering. Everyone can do something about it; they can love. You can share love. You can be God's language.

I spoke earlier of my sister. She is now seventy. During our visit she said "We have the money to buy a bigger home, but Doug and Janey, who are blind, would be disoriented. Besides, we all love this house. We don't need much, and we have each other."

Pete, age seventy-six, farms one and one-half acres of garden. Frieda takes Doug and Janey daily to the Orange Grove school in Chattanooga, Tennessee. Doug and Janey live with more love than most people ever get the opportunity to experience. Human beings are God's language.

On the trip back from Chattanooga, I did not feel, "How pathetic. How cruel life has been to them." Frieda said, "I wish I could invite my friends here to spend some time, but I don't think they would be comfortable." I did not feel, "God is unjust." I felt, "How fortunate they are to share a simple life of love, protection, and understanding." Brooke, my granddaughter, was not squeamish or intimidated by the loud and animated behavior of Doug and Janey. On the contrary, she was warm and affectionate. She sat for pictures with them. When Doug got a little too loud, she patted him on the knee. Human beings are God's language.

Frieda, Pete, Doug, and Janey are God's language. When bad things happen to good people, you do something about it. You become God's language of love.

Notes

1. Harold S. Kushner, *When Bad Things Happen to Good People* (New York: Avon Books, 1981), 22.

2. Cited in ibid., 118.

26

Diggin' Up Bones

This past week, our mayor was to be on a radio talk-show. He was forty-five minutes late. During that time, the disc jockeys played "Diggin' Up Bones" by Randy Travis. The mayor has had his travails. He told them Jesus would forgive him. He has even been on Donahue because of his extramarital behavior. Some people live and regret it. Some people regret that they haven't lived it. Which is worse?

The Mariner I space probe was launched from Cape Canaveral on July 28, 1962, toward Venus. After thirteen minutes of flight, a booster engine would give acceleration up to 25,820 m.p.h.; after forty-four minutes, 9,000 solar cells would unfold; after eighty days, a computer would calculate the final course corrections; and after one hundred days the craft would circle the unknown planet, scanning the mysterious cloud in which it is bathed. However, with an efficiency that is truly disheartening, Mariner I plunged into the Atlantic Ocean only four minutes after take-off. Inquires later revealed that a minus sign had been omitted from the instructions fed into the computer. "It was human error," a launch spokesman said. The minus sign cost 45,280,000 hours and $12 million.

Some People Live to Regret It

If anyone ever had a reason for holding a grudge against God, it would be Dave Dravecky. On November 13, 1989, he announced his retirement from baseball. A tumor in his pitching arm resulted in two serious breaks. He pitched seven years for the San Fransico Giants. One of the most dramatic games I ever saw was when the Giants played Montreal during his comeback, but it was short lived.

The scoreboard flashed: "Welcome Back Dave." He fell and broke his arm again. With Will Clark over him, he writhed in pain, "Oh, gosh, Will, it hurts. It's killing me! It's broke. It's broke. It feels like I've broken my arm." Later he said, "The hardest part of the last two years has been the uncertainty. I had to learn to do what was within my grasp, one day at a time, and leave control of the rest trustingly to God. Perhaps most of all, I've learned to put my life in God's hands." "Forgive us our debts, as we also have forgiven our debtors" (Matt. 6:12).

One of the most haunting statements I ever read came from Lewis Smede's book, *Forgive and Forget:* "Some only pretend forgiveness in order to punish with righteous mercy." Another is more appropriate: "You cannot change the past—but you can let God heal the hurt."

Four Stages of Forgiveness

Smedes says there are four stages in forgiveness: hurt, hate, healing, and coming together.

Hurt

In 1982 my book *Burnout in Ministry* was released. I was looking for rave reviews. One publicity specialist sent me three dozen reviews. Only one was negative, but it was the only one that sticks in my memory.

It read: "If Faulkner did not work for the Sunday School Board, it would not be published. The research is skimpy. The development is sophomoric." I was crushed. Isn't it remarkable how memorable a few negative words can become? *Hurt* means to be taken in as a friend but then treated as a dog.

It is personal.—You cannot believe the phrase *nothing personal* because hurt is always personal.

Unfair.—Being yelled at for hitting your sister is fair. Being screamed at by a drunken father is unfair. The drunk won't remember. The person yelled at will.

Deep.—It cuts past the layers of protection into the scalp of long-lasting and deep hurt.

Why do people hurt us? Some think we deserve it. Some are simply obsessive-compulsive people who are *out-of-control*. These are the ones who "turn it all loose." They "tell people off." They "dump on people." They are children who are still fed on milk and not meat. They win pity, not respect. Some are *spillovers* from other problems. In therapy, it is called *displacement*. Displacing anger in one place after accumulating it from another. Does the Bible say forgive others, except when they hurt you? Of course it doesn't. Forgive others, except when they have abused you? Of course it doesn't. In Matthew 18:21, it tells how many times you should forgive your brother. Up to seven times? No, seventy times seven. Some translations say seventy-seven. The answer is still interminable. *Forgiveness is a behavior, not an act.* Why do we talk about forgiveness so often? Because it is so often needed.

Forgive and forget. "Get rid of all bitterness, rage and anger, brawling and slander, along with every form of malice. Be kind and compassionate to one another, forgiving each other, just as in Christ God forgave you" (Eph. 4:31-32).

Annoyances don't need forgiveness, just tolerance. Fifteen items are taken into a ten-item line at the supermarket. That is an annoyance. Switching channels is an annoyance. Not noticing someone when he walks by is an annoyance. Snubbing is another.

Disloyalty, though, requires forgiveness. Putting someone down to embarrass them is more than annoyance. Betrayal requires forgiveness. Peter required forgiveness. Judas required forgiveness. Brutality requires forgiveness. Adultery is brutally inflicted pain. Child abuse is brutally inflicted pain. But each requires forgiveness.

Hate

Love your neighbor, and hate your enemy? No, love your enemies. Do good to them. How is that possible? Love sin and be judged. Loving the sinner and hating the sin is more righteous. Tell me how you did it. You can hate passively by ignoring someone. You can hate actively. "I have to get this off my chest." I have yet to see dumping activate redemption. It alienates. The alternative is own your own anger. Anger means we are alive and well. However, hate is a sign of sickness and the need for healing.

To add to the dilemma, we most often aim our hatred at people who live within the circle of our committed love—the people who have been loyal or we expect to be loyal. That is why it hurts so deeply to be betrayed by people in a church.

In Michael Christopher's play, *The Black Angel,* Herman Engel was a German general in World War II and sentenced by the Nuremberg Court to thirty years in prison for atrocities. He was released and settled in a village. Morrieaux, a French journalist in the village, had lost his whole family. He stoked up the fanatics, and they decided to burn Engel's cabin. Morrieaux went to Engel hoping to bait him with the impending danger but found a tired old confused man. Morrieaux changed his mind and offered help. "Not unless you forgive me," Engel replied. He couldn't. Engel and his wife were shot, and their house burned. Morrieaux's hate could not set him free. Sometimes hate only nibbles at the edges of the heart: It does not always burn out the lining of the soul, but sometimes is a carcinoma.

Heal

Healing can only come with the insight into our wrong, sin, and new feeling of healing. It need not be spontaneous. I have heard some say, "You are not a Christian unless you can find instantaneous forgiveness." That is like saying there is no healing of cancer over a two-year period. There must be instant healing, or it is not healing. That is preposterous. Absence of instantaneous healing to some is a lack of faith. Forgiveness of hurt and hate can take place, but it is not always easy. Insight into our own sin is first. Then a new feeling comes. There is a process of transferring the hurt to God first. He can take it. He is bigger than our hurt. You may say, "If God had not let this happen, I would not be hurt." Then transfer that to forgiveness. God can help us heal.

Paul Tillich wrote, "Genuine forgiveness is participation, reunion overcoming the power of estrangement." This means you have not forgiven unless you are reconciled in an intimate relationship. However, some people bring too much damage to each other to live together. A wife can forgive an abusive husband but still be better off without him if he continues to harm her and the children. You need not expose yourself to the abusive onslaught of brutality to prove forgiveness.

Come Together

Here is the key: Both parties must bring about an honest coming together, not just one of them. They must know the reality of what they did to hurt. They must feel the hurt that you felt.

In *Forgive and Forget,* Smedes tells the story of a rigid preacher who abused his daughter sexually until she was seventeen and left home. The man convinced his daughter that a father who lived close to God could do no wrong. Later, she is freed from her hate, but she knows she cannot take him back in the same way. She cannot be a child again.

If he has Alzheimer's disease and she is to take care of him, can they come together in a forgiving relationship? Only God can give her that power. She can not conjure up that power on her own. She must start over.

Some people are hard to forgive: Those who pour salt in the wound *and won't let it heal* seemingly enjoy the vision of humiliation. This is evil.

Those who are invisible, such as a mother who forsakes a child. Does she do it because she loves or doesn't love? Only she knows, but she is hard to forgive. The parent who died. Why did she leave you? Only God knows the answer. You can choose to hold on to that grudge toward a dead parent for the rest of your life as many do or to let it go.

Those who do not deserve it—who impact hurt out of their own character flaw. The irrational "floating anger" person spews poison on impulse—get it off my chest. Like a cancer, it will fester again. The abusive spouse makes the other responsible for any pain they feel. "Why are you late?" "Why can't you be more thoughtful?" "When are you going to bring in more money?" "Why don't you take the responsibility for the failures of our children?"

Those who do not care are the prodigals. Those who abandon the loved ones who matter and expect God to forgive at the last minute. God does, but a person finds it difficult and sometimes virtually impossible to forgive those who do not care.

And finally, ourselves. The pain we cause other people becomes the hate we feel for ourselves for having done them wrong. In Dostoevski's novel, *Crime and Punishment,* Raskolnikov murdered a helpless woman and an old pawnbroker, and his guilt was overbearing. He could not forgive himself and tried to excuse himself.

Raskolnikov could not find forgiveness until he quit rationalizing and excusing himself. He would always have guilt as long as he protected himself from the pain of shame and self-remorse. You need a clear head to make way for your forgiving heart. Remember self-esteem is not the same as self-forgiveness. The first is the discovery of your own excellence and then you discover your own faults. In a strange way, it is a compliment to be the recipient of those who unleash their poison on us for whatever reason. They would be more considerate of a mentally retarded person, child, or helpless person, but they consider us strong enough to take it. So in a sense, it is a compliment. Most of us are too brittle to release the untamed venom of hurt we dump on ourselves. Ordinary people do extraordinary evil, so do we, but we still need forgiveness. Some people use cruelty as a way of coping. They need forgiveness. Ephesians 4:32 says, "Be kind and compassionate to one another, forgiving each other, just as in Christ God forgave you." Hebrews 9:22 says, "Without the shedding of blood there is no forgiveness." The price must be paid; the rent must be paid. First John 1:9 says, "If we confess our sins, he is faithful and just and will forgive us our sins and purify us from all unrighteousness."

Stop diggin' up bones. Forgive others. Forgive yourself.